Have a Little Faith

THE REVEREND KATE BOTTLEY

PENGUIN LIFE

AN IMPRINT OF

PENGUIN BOOKS

PENGUIN LIFE

UK | USA | Canada | Ireland | Australia
India | New Zealand | South Africa

Penguin Life is part of the Penguin Random House group of companies
whose addresses can be found at global.penguinrandomhouse.com.

First published 2023
001

Copyright © Kate Bottley 2023

The moral right of the author has been asserted

Set in 13.5/16pt Garamond MT Std
Typeset by Jouve (UK), Milton Keynes
Printed and bound in Great Britain by Clays Ltd, Elcograf S.p.A.

The authorized representative in the EEA is Penguin Random House Ireland,
Morrison Chambers, 32 Nassau Street, Dublin D02 YH68

A CIP catalogue record for this book is available from the British Library

ISBN: 978-0-241-60566-0

www.greenpenguin.co.uk

For
Mum
(and Wilki)

Contents

Introduction

One of the many funny things about being a reverend is that people expect you to talk about your beliefs all the time. I suspect that for lots of people who don't have a faith, it's also one of the greatest worries about hanging out with a reverend.

This is never more apparent to me than when I'm travelling on a train – something I do a lot more of these days, now that I'm also a television and radio presenter. Wearing a dog collar means I can pretty much always bag a double seat to myself on a train. I reckon people think if they sit next to me I'll start talking to them about the Bible, so they sit anywhere else but next to me. It's true, I do like to talk about my faith, but let me ask you this: do you want to talk about your job when you're on the train home after a long day? Or would you rather chat about last night's *Bake Off*? Or just not chat at all?

That's not to say I don't also attract certain people when I'm on public transport. I seem to be a magnet for folk who have strong feelings about alien abduction, or those who think I should join their far-right political movement. I confess that sometimes in those sorts of situations the collar gets quietly slipped off and hidden in my handbag. Although sometimes I do the opposite, and taking the commandment about 'loving your neigh-bour' as seriously as I do, the most loving thing I can do for my neighbours in the train carriage is keep alien-loving strangers chatting so they don't bother anyone else.

Just like those people who are suspicious of me on trains, you are probably expecting me to tell you some stories from the Bible and give you at least a few high-lights from Christianity in this book, and you won't be disappointed! But don't worry, there are plenty of other non-Bible-related stories too (even one about me and Clare Balding on *The Wheel*), so you really do get your bang for your buck. The truth is that my faith has played a part in most of my adult life, my belief has guided me through life's ups and downs and made me who I am, so there is not one without the other. And that's what I'm all about, showing that faith plays a part in a normal life, and vice versa.

I'm a fully paid-up Christian, so the only faith I really know how to talk about at any length is Christianity. And I would never presume to try to explain someone else's faith to you, or them. But I think I should clarify here that, for me, the Bible isn't a rulebook or a set of instruc-tions, it's much more important than that. In my eyes, it's a collection of useful (and admittedly sometimes slightly bonkers) stories, that each new generation can think about and interpret as they need. I take the Bible far too seriously to take it literally. You don't have to be a Chris-tian to be inspired by and learn from the Bible, it's a document that has informed our culture and is the basis of many societies; even if you don't see it as a sacred text, it is an influential one. And you don't need to know the Bible, or any other religious text, off by heart, to have a bit of faith.

So, yes, this book is about faith, but it's also just about being human, because believing in things is part and parcel of our existence. I promise not to go on too much about that time Jesus went to a wedding, or when Noah built an ark, or Jacob made his favourite son a shiny new robe. You can read the Bible yourself without me telling you what's in it. What you'll get instead (as well as a few nuggets of wisdom from the Bible) is some thoughts on how we can benefit from faith today, in the twenty-first century, at a time when science has proven so many of the Bible's stories to be impossible, and so many of us are wondering what the future holds for the human race.

What is faith?

First, I'd like to say that faith is a really normal thing. OK, so perhaps some of the stories within the Christian faith, like men who can walk on water and come back from the dead, are anything but normal. But it's worth remembering that most countries in the world still have a belief of some sort at their core. In fact, most of the world is part of a religion. In the affluent West, we've perhaps lost sight of our faith more than in other places. Or perhaps what I mean is, we've seen our faith morph into something different – we're not so hot on organized, church-based religion any more, on doctrine and prescribed viewpoints, but we've become incredibly good at following influencers, we're passionate about our football teams and we still tell our children that a man called Santa brings their presents down the chimney every December, but only if they're good. I suspect our distancing from organized religion also has something to do with us not seeming to need God in the same way that we once did. Improvements in health and social care mean life isn't always as fragile as it once was. We've also seen a rise in the idea of the individual and that individual's needs and desires, which doesn't always fit in with the concept of organized, established faith.

The point for me is that faith isn't about what or who we believe in, it's that *believing in something* is what humans have always done. It's part of our story and in our DNA. Why? Because when it comes down to it, having faith in something makes us feel connected. It makes us feel like we matter. Faith means we are in it together, that we believe we will be OK and things will get better.

Some people argue that we have less faith today because we now know so much, we no longer need a God. But I like to think that science and faith are not mutually exclusive; we don't need to choose between them. We've just been so busy concentrating on the science bit that we've not exercised our faith muscles in a while. They're weak, and we're not sure how they work any more. But for me, there is no reason why human beings can't believe in science and still have some kind of faith. Science is awe-inspiring, after all. How can we not have faith in the face of such incredible discoveries and knowledge?

And the stuff of belief doesn't only belong to those of us who wear a collar or call ourselves Reverend. In fact, I'll let you into a not-so-secret secret: most of the people who have dog collars around their necks will struggle to believe in all their faith, all the time. I may have the degrees and the certificates to say I'm bona fide religious, but often I am no more or less qualified than anyone else to talk about the things of faith. It's called faith, it's not called absolute certainty.

Another secret: almost all the problems that relate to religion, whether it's wars over countries or the control of women's bodies, are caused because those in positions of authority are trying to control others, somehow. Just as it does in politics, power does funny things to people, even to the religious.

Wherever you sit on the faith spectrum, I'm here to tell you it's OK. It's OK to only want to pray sometimes, or to try to make a deal with the God you don't believe in only when things are really desperate or you need a big favour. It's OK to say you're not religious, but still want to have some sort of ceremony or ritual at your wedding or your funeral; when the big stuff in life happens. It's really OK to feel a bit weird in a church, even though you're pretty sure it's all nonsense, and want to light a candle, or to cry at the ethereal power of the Queen's funeral. It's OK to say you don't believe any of it, but to also hope that there is something intangible and unnamed, beyond and bigger than anything we can see or hear or touch. Having a faith, no matter how fledgling or small, no matter how fragile or unquantifiable, is nothing to feel embarrassed or awkward about. It doesn't always need to be explained, or justified or even public. If faith, even a little of it, makes putting your feet on the floor in the morning a little easier, then why should anyone deny themselves the comfort and reassurance it might bring?

I often use the analogy of a Venn diagram to explain what I think it means to be human, what sets us apart from other animals on earth. Imagine three circles. They each represent a different element of our quest to feel fulfilled and whole. The first is all about you. The good news is this is one topic you're already the world-renowned expert in; nobody knows more. The first, and probably most obvious part of our quest to feel human is to be as well connected with yourself as possible, developing your expertise in knowing yourself as well as you can. Know yourself in terms of your mental, physical and spiritual health. What are your good bits? What do you do well? What are your shortcomings?

The second circle is all about other people. They are more of a mystery, but to be human is to make connections with others, whether that's through friendship, family or even just an exchange with a delivery driver. Human beings connect with other human beings; we do it to survive and to grow and thrive. 'No man is an island,' said the poet John Donne. I couldn't agree more.

The third circle is something more difficult to understand than ourselves or other humans. It is the thing that is bigger than us. I call it God, but you might use other words and terms, or even no words at all. Time and space stretching out above, below, before and beyond, connection with the 'wow'. You might have heard whispers of it when someone was born or died, or on a mountain top, or while taking heavy medication, or you may have done the 12 steps and call it your 'higher power'. Your rational brain might explain it away and that's fine, because this sense of otherness is often so intangible that comprehension of it is thoroughly impossible, but at some point in life you will feel it.

Now you have these three circles – self, others and Other (I call it God) – put them together in a Venn diagram and the bit in the middle is the sweet spot, the part where connectedness with self, others and divine overlaps; it's here that faith sits and where meaning is found.

I don't expect us to achieve spiritual Nirvana together over the next few chapters, but it's my hope that thinking about how those connections are made in your life, and how they are nurtured and developed, might just help. Because faith has helped me navigate some of the most difficult bits of being alive. Sometimes it has actually made my life harder, but more often than not, it has helped me find my way through so many of the messy, messed-up complexities of human existence.

I'm going to share some stories, to tell you what I've learned, and suggest a few things to do, to help you to develop your faith muscles and find your own sweet spot.

Mind the gap

When it comes to organized religion, the numbers speak for themselves. In the UK, the 2021 Census showed that the number of people identifying as Christian was down from 59.3 per cent in 2011, to 46.2 per cent in 2021. And it's not just the Christians. Numbers for the other five major world religions – Sikhism, Hinduism, Judaism, Islam and Buddhism (although technically Buddhism isn't a religion, it's a philosophy) – that coexist with Christianity in the UK fluctuate, but the general shift for all of them is down. That 46.2 per cent still equates to a whopping 27.5 million people, but asked the question, 'Do you believe in God?' I suspect most people in the UK are now a 'No'.

I think a big reason for this is because lots of people have beliefs that don't fall under those categories of old, and there isn't a box for 'spiritual' or 'I believe in something but I don't know what', which is sad. But I think the main reason for this decline is that the language of religion is not being spoken. The stories of faith are not being told. Religion is becoming an ancient tongue, like Latin. As the gap between religion (the original speakers) and the rest of society (the non-speakers) gets wider and wider, the two find it increasingly difficult to understand each other. We need interpreters, which is where I come in.

Let me give you an example. Fifteen years ago there was a big debate raging in the Christian church around women bishops. I was booked to speak at a public debate about the issue. Wanting to look my best as I argued my point, I went to my hairdresser. As she cut my hair she asked the inevitable question, 'Are you going out tonight?'

'Yes,' I replied, 'I'm going to take part in a debate on women bishops.'

'Nice. What's a bishop?' she asked.

At the beginning of the twentieth century, even up to perhaps the end of that century, this question would have been inconceivable. Everyone knew what a bishop was. But here was someone who had not ever been taken to church or been immersed in church culture. She hadn't seen a bishop discussed on television or in pop culture either. Why should she know what a bishop is?

Before I was a vicar I was a teacher. I remember asking my class of white, working-class fourteen-year-olds to tell me who the main people in the Nativity story were. Not one could mention more than baby Jesus. There was no Mary, no Joseph, no shepherds, no angels. I'm not complaining here, or expressing outrage that these kids didn't know their Bible. Why should they when it's not what they believe? Nor am I suggesting that education has failed them. Teachers have got enough on their plates – I know. What I am saying is that religion (all and any religion) is not part of most people's frame of reference these days. As a Christian belonging to the established state religion, I can no longer presume a level of cultural Christianity. A friend who is a university lecturer tells me of countless students who miss the references to faith in Shakespeare and Chaucer. Another who teaches art history has to start with stories of what the Crucifixion was before they can look at any of the religious art of the Renaissance. We are simply not as religious as we used to be. But does that mean we have lost the need for faith?

Sometimes I describe myself as a curator of faith conversations, by which I mean I see it as my job to try and speak into that increasingly wide gap between everyday culture and faith. I believe that humans still need the stuff of faith, and that belief can inform hope. It's just that perhaps we've tied faith up so closely with things our scientifically enlightened minds can't believe, or that we think we have to believe all of it, rather than some of it, that it feels impossible to separate out the stuff which is helpful from the stuff which is at best unhelpful and at worst downright damaging.

What you might think I think

You can be religious and not believe in all of religion. In fact, if total, outright belief is the qualifier, then I think

I've failed. The truth is, some days I'm not sure if I believe any of it, let alone all of it.

Now it's true I am a card-carrying member of the Christian religion, I describe myself as Christian, I would tick the Christian box on the Census form. I used to be a teacher. But I'm also a mum, a wife, a rugby player, a television and radio presenter, a pint-drinker and a wild-swimmer, among many, many other things. All these aspects of me inform who I am and how I feel about, and lean into, my faith. So it's sometimes funny when people tell me what they think I think about things, because very often I'm thinking the opposite.

A few years ago I wrote an article about gender pronouns for God, for the *Guardian* newspaper. Now, I'm very careful around pronouns for God and I hope you'll notice as you read this book that I tend not to use them at all. It's not that I think God is a woman, I don't, but I don't think God is a man either. Nor do I think they are non-binary. I think God is all of those things but also none of them. I believe God is utterly unique, like nothing else in the universe, incomparable, indescribable, it is beyond the sufficiency of the human language to articulate what and who God is, he and she are too small and binary terms for God.

But that doesn't stop us trying. And so we call God 'he', we talk of Father and Shepherd, Lord and King, when God is none of those, but also all of them. We think of a physical being in a physical place because we *are* physical beings in a physical place, and we can't comprehend the incomprehensible. I wrote all of these thoughts for the *Guardian*, a respected, national broadsheet newspaper. I wasn't prepared for the shock it caused. What did I mean I didn't believe in an old man on a cloud with a beard who controls the weather and lives behind a golden gate in the sky?

So much of our spirituality, theology and understanding of God becomes 'set' in our primary school years. Ask a six-year-old and a sixty-year-old to draw 'God' and they'll probably draw something very similar to my cosmic Santa. We don't take our personal perception of God beyond the thinking of our infancy because we've never really needed to. We revisit the metaphors at key moments, especially death, when we hope for our loved one to be welcomed into the heaven we imagined as a child, but we haven't for a minute thought what that might look like using our own adult understanding. I'm not dismissing a childlike faith here, rather that unlike our other beliefs and values, our thoughts on what God is don't seem to grow up, we are stuck on the celestial Father Christmas. So, if you're asking me if I believe in that God, the one I met in primary school, I don't.

So when I'm talking to other people about faith, it's a challenge for me when they make assumptions about what I believe. Faith is not homogenized. If you want to belong to a religion then there are a few common creeds and tenets you verbally sign up to, but even then us humans do like to interpret what those might mean. So, for example, to be a Christian you have to believe in the resurrection of Jesus, but even then you'll get those who don't think that was a historic event, but rather symbolic. It's the same with the virgin birth. Of course this breadth of beliefs is what makes it so brilliant to have faith, but also what makes it so challenging. It might sound strange to you, but it's no surprise to me that the most common fall-outs I have are with other Christians. You might also assume I am pro-life, anti-gay, anti-drugs and every other pious belief you can name. The truth is you will find Christians who are those things, and you will find Christians who are not. The community of the religious reflects society as a whole; not everyone thinks the same thing and also not forever. I change my mind about my beliefs. I don't have the same faith I had five years ago; I don't know where my faith will be in the next five minutes. I grow, I change, I question, I come to deeper or different understanding. As a culture we're not great at accepting that people change their minds, but I like to think that change is growth. Be very suspicious of folk who are always certain and sure; in my experience they are more scared and unsure than any of us.

What I actually think

So, in summary, I don't have faith in my faith all the time and I change my mind a lot. Why should you bother reading this book, I hear you ask? I don't think I've got all the answers, even though I am very chatty, but I do know that as a modern vicar with years of experience, a day job on the telly and radio and a family who keep me on my toes, I have a unique perspective on faith today.

I meet so many people in my work, many of them in church but just as many outside it, and it strikes me that despite the myriad ways in which we can all stay connected, more of us are feeling more isolated than ever. In the past (and still today), the physical church building served to bring communities together, for warmth and worship, company and food. Now we don't have a common belief in the same way, we've lost the coming together in our communities that the formal church of the past might have given us. I don't want to deny progress or suggest we go back to an old way of doing things – I love my social media too much for that – but I do believe that we need to allow ourselves to grasp and hold on to the parts of faith that work for us, whether that's lighting a candle, singing songs, saying a prayer, marking turning points in each year, or simply coming together to celebrate in love, and death.

Without religion we don't have the language to make sense of the deep, meaningful things that happen to us in life. We're scared of things going wrong, of not knowing what our purpose is, of people dying, because there isn't a way of talking about it. I do a lot of funerals and I've noticed fewer people are going to see the bodies of their loved ones who have died, sometimes because they are scared. But many people still like to touch the coffin, because they want to feel like they are still connected somehow. That's their faith. And that's OK.

I think we need a new understanding of what it means to be spiritual, so that we can have these conversations around the big themes in life without fear of being judged. As a vicar today, I want to be an interpreter in those conversations, and to help you find the support and inspiration you need in life's all-important moments.

In the following pages you'll find chapters on some of the big themes in life, from the obvious ones like love and death to the slightly less immediate, but equally challenging ones like success and loneliness. I've had my own struggles with all of them, and seen others struggle through them too, so I wanted to share what I've learned along the way in the hope that it might provide some guidance or comfort when you need it most.

These themes mean different things to different people, because life is full of contradictions. Faith is also full of contradictions: it's a 'sure and certain hope' after all, which more often than not is neither sure nor certain. It can all be very confusing. It's my hope that after reading this book, you might find yourself feeling a little less confused, and a little more curious about exploring your own sense of faith. And, if faith is something you've been out of touch with for a while, that you might feel more comfortable in reconnecting with it, however and whenever feels right for you.

So go on, see what you think, there's no need to be scared. Just have a little faith.

1. Success

If you saw me on *Gogglebox* or follow me on social media you probably already know that I watch a lot of telly. It goes on first thing in the morning and gets switched off last thing at night. There's a middle-class snobbery about folk who love telly. But I don't agree with that. Telly is marvellous. And although I know I don't need to justify it, it's also where I do a lot of my learning and where I find a lot of places to reflect.

Some shows are better than others at providing opportunities for reflection, although you might be surprised by some of my favourites. *Love Island*, *Naked Attraction* and *The Wheel* have all provided material for my *Pause for Thought* broadcasts on Radio 2, and sermon illustrations. One of my favourite recent TV series was *Fleabag*, starring Phoebe Waller Bridge. There's a scene where Fleabag is teasing her sister, Claire, about doing something unspeakable in a sink when she's caught short. Claire defends herself by saying: 'I have two degrees, a husband and a Burberry coat.' As if those things are a clear indication of her success.

My daughter, Ruby, has turned this line into a kind of life quote and mutters it at me, usually when I'm being ridiculous about how busy and important I am. I have a husband, I have two degrees, I don't yet own a Burberry coat (although I am watching two second-hand ones on eBay at the moment). I think I'm quite successful. I certainly don't fail very much, if failure is the opposite of success. I've passed almost all the exams I've ever sat. I have most of the material things that might be associated with success: a good job, a nice house, a car. I'm married, I can't say always happily but mostly content. I've got two grown-up children, who as far as I know haven't killed anyone, yet. I guess I'm successful but, if I'm honest, I'm not really sure that's how it should be measured.

It's fair to say that when I was growing up, expectations of me and what I would 'do' were always, what I'd call, realistic. I was the youngest child and only daughter (my brother David is four years older than me) of a solidly working-class family. Our terraced house on Freedom Road in Sheffield still had an outside loo when I was young. We did have an indoor bathroom, but the outside toilet was still in use and became a kind of den for my brother and me. It was great, you never had to go in when you were out playing, like a really cold en-suite for the backyard. The house didn't get central heating until I was in junior school. Success as it is generally understood nowadays – a university education and a job you like, big house, long-haul holidays and all that – it wasn't a thing in my world. For my parents and the community I grew up in, success looked like something far less expensive. It meant marriage and kids, a job for life, and if you were

really successful, being able to keep up with paying your
mortgage or even one day pay it off altogether.

For girls in particular, success wasn't something for us
to concern ourselves with. As a girl I was raised to not
make a show of myself, to not make too much of a fuss
or make myself the centre of attention. I didn't find this
easy. Women still had very clearly defined roles, and
while we were expected to be hardworking, we were also
not meant to have ideas above our station. To blow your
own trumpet about stuff you were good at or could do
was to be a big-head. No one wanted to be called a big-
head. If my mum and dad were going out with another
couple the men sat in the front and the women in the
back. My mum and her sisters didn't learn to drive until
they were in their forties.

Success is often defined by what someone does for a
job or how good they are at the job they do. And certainly,
you can be a desperately unsuccessful but well-earning
investment banker and a thoroughly skint but incredibly
successful production line worker, if you measure success
in more than financial terms. Like most people, I had all
sorts of jobs that I wasn't very successful at when I was
younger. I worked in a shop in Meadowhall for a while, as
a Saturday girl. I was supposed to keep my eye out for
shoplifters. I spotted loads but was always far too scared
to challenge them. Then I washed up in a pub for a couple
of weeks – I was terrible at that. I was bored within two
minutes and rubbish at scouring. I went on to work in a
sausage factory, twirling phallic Cumberlands into tight

coils and skewering them for barbecues, wrapping bacon around chipolatas for pigs in blankets. It's a straightforward job by anyone else's standards but I managed to lock myself in the giant walk-in fridge, more than once, and was tricked by my fellow employees into asking the supervisor for both stripy paint and a long weight. Clearly my success wasn't to be found on the factory floor or the sticky carpets of a pub; I wouldn't have minded if they were, and certainly the experience of those jobs wasn't wasted, but my path lay elsewhere.

Years later, as a newly qualified priest, I took my parents on the train to London, so that they could see me preach at Westminster Abbey. I noticed my mum, Margaret, crying and looking very worried on the journey. I asked her what she was worried about – after all, it was me who was preaching at Westminster Abbey, not her – and she asked tearfully: 'What if I show you up?' I had been not only the first woman but the first person in my family to go to university and get a degree. My mum left school at fifteen with no qualifications, and my grandma on my dad's side never really learned to read. Somehow in that simple, heartbreaking question it brought home to me in far greater clarity the distance that I had travelled from my childhood to this moment.

Despite that realization many years ago at the start of my career in the clergy, I am only now beginning to step into the thought that I am good enough, that I am good at what I do, and that it is even OK to say that out loud sometimes. It's difficult to see what you do well when often the narrative has been not to 'show off' or be 'big-headed' and it's only through the encouragement of others over the years that I've been able to start believing in myself. When I have these thoughts I'm reminded of the story of the woman at the well, in John's Gospel. She's one of my favourite women in the Bible. She was obviously a bit of an outcast or had at least done something unspeakable, as she wasn't at the well in the morning with the other women, but at lunchtime when no one else was there because it was unbearably hot. While she's getting her water, Jesus turns up and asks her for a drink, which is pretty jaw-dropping in itself because she's an unclean Samaritan woman on her own and he's an educated Jewish super-rabbi who teaches people important stuff – he shouldn't be drinking out of the same cup as her! But she engages him in conversation, chats and they get into a big theological debate.

Instead of feeling ashamed or intimidated, she owns her story and stands out there in the midday heat, giving him a run for his money on some of the big issues of the day. Even when his disciple mates show up and ask Jesus what he thinks he's doing talking to her, she remains unashamedly herself in that moment. She steps into who she is and owns it. On the face of it she has little status or success, she is inconsequential, but that doesn't stop her shaping her own story rather than allowing it to be shaped for her.

I think herein lies something about the secret to success. Success isn't perhaps how others measure it but rather about how you measure it yourself. That success is grounded and rooted in confidence and ownership of your own narrative. Sometimes when I doubt my own successes, I remind myself of her and I think what a bloody great woman she must have been, and how I'd really like to go day drinking with her in the afterlife.

So, in many ways you could say I'm successful. I've come from really humble beginnings and I'm on the telly, which means I'm 'famous'. Fame, even if I'm not quite an A-lister, is sometimes used as a measure of success. It's true people sometimes stop me for a selfie in Morrison's, accompanied with the inevitable line, 'My mum loves you.' I'm also trusted with a public role in an established institution, the national church, and God trusts me to be a sort of 'area manager' here on earth. And yet, if the distance I have travelled means success, does that do a disservice to the successes of my parents and the generations before them, who survived wars and poverty, left school without qualifications and held down multiple jobs to feed their families, all at a time when children still died of scarlet fever and you had a bath once a week if you were lucky? If I'm successful, they had superpowers.

My family certainly think I'm successful – and I think they are. Perhaps success is something we measure and acknowledge in others and not ourselves, something that constantly appears just out of reach or belonging to someone else. And here lies a road to torment and madness.

The comparison trap

The old saying 'comparison is the thief of joy' is a help-ful reminder that this path of thought is an emotional cul-de-sac. But it is irresistible. The way we define our-selves as humans is grounded and rooted in comparison. It's the only way to measure everything from exam grade boundaries to the Olympics and even fashion. We look around, see what others are doing, attempt initially to mimic and then exceed. It's caused me problems over the years. This constant need to be the best, to beat others, to be successful, to win. It's not so much that I'm competitive as that I just don't like losing.

One of my favourite quiz shows is Richard Osman's *House of Games*; if you haven't seen it I heartily recom-mend it to you. I was delighted when I was asked to be on it. I don't think I'm giving the game away too much when I say that, despite it being a nightly show, each week is actually all filmed in one day. I went in all guns blazing. I smashed the first game, leaving my fellow competitors many points behind – Richard said I had the biggest lead ever in the show. Being filmed over one day means a quick change and then on to the next. By the time the end of the day came I couldn't be certain what day of the week it was at all. Five outfit changes, five pairs of shoes, five slightly different make-up and hair looks. Although as with most things television, the cis men seem to have it easier. The blokes I was on with just changed their shirts. If you look very closely on the programme you'll see that most of the chaps are wearing the same socks every day for a week. I won, by the way. I like winning. In fact I was so pleased with myself that a kindly member of the crew pulled me to one side and suggested I might like to 'rein it in a little'.

But I can't help myself. Sometimes it's not enough that I win, others must lose, in this case Joel Dommett, Yolanda Brown and John Thomson. I hate this about myself. Comparison – the yardstick to how successful we are – is a dangerous tool, if allowed to rage unchecked and uncontrolled. It means that success is not just measured by our own achievements but also by others' failures. I find I am still prone to measure myself against the successes of others. Especially as a woman (am I beautiful enough?), especially as a mother (am I motherly enough?), and especially as a mother to a child with special needs (is my family normal enough?); the ways in which my family and its challenges differ from everyone else's are never far from my mind – more on this later. It's not always easy to remember, but focusing on what others have, and how it compares to what you have, will almost never leave you feeling remotely successful. It's probably my worst kept secret that I would like to have a bash at *Strictly Come Dancing*, but at the same time I know that it could be disastrous for my mental health because the show is all about comparison, success and popularity. The thought of Craig Revel Horwood holding one of those paddles up with a three on it would certainly send me into a spiral of self-loathing.

So although I might have some of the hallmarks of a successful person, it's all relative. Where I'm from I've done pretty well for myself, but the wider image of success often seems to be synonymous with material wealth and an impressive career, the never-ending achievement of things and a good set of cheekbones. Think of anyone you consider to be successful and they'll probably have done quite nicely for themselves. They'll probably have achieved a bunch of impressive things, and look pretty good on it, too. But we have to remind ourselves that everyone's starting point is different, and that things could change any moment. By the metric our society measures success with, I think it looks like being pretty extraordinary, so I've learned to measure success on my own terms.

Sharing success

After doctors and therapists (beauty and the other sort), vicars are afforded more insight into people's private lives than most other jobs, and one of the things I've learned from working so closely within a community is that the success of an individual is almost always the result of the support of others. Recently when Jamie Lee Curtis accepted her Oscar she said in her speech, 'Look kids, WE won an Oscar, look MOM and DAD, we won an Oscar'; those who are awarded and applauded are just the representatives of not only the teams that helped make it happen but also the generations that went before which set the context for the subsequent achievement. And here is perhaps where we might see success as not being at the expense of someone else and as a result of someone being beaten and others being better, but rather as an individual's success being shared by others.

Think of a time perhaps where you passed an exam or won a race or even cooked a great meal. You were able to do that because of a team of others along the way who supported you to achieve it. So does being successful always mean standing head and shoulders above everyone else? After all, plenty of us are on what I call the B-team. And by B I really mean Bee, as in bumble, or worker. What's the B-team? For me it's the people who make sure the door is unlocked at church, and that the water's warm when I am doing a christening. It's also the person who fills the shelves at the supermarket, empties the bins, or delivers our vaccines. It's everyone who is out there getting on with their work, playing their part, being the cogs in the wheel. Without them we'd none of us be successful, and yet we so rarely acknowledge their achievements.

The fifth-century orthodox theologian St John Chrysostom wrote: 'The bee is honoured above all other animals, not because she labours but because she labours for others.' People on the B-team work hard in the background, quietly doing what they do to benefit others, and just like the buzzy bee they too can sometimes be overlooked.

I suspect the antidote to my need to crush others in order to prove myself successful lies in acknowledging how much any success I have isn't dependent entirely on my own hard work or skill but in a large part on the wisdom and skill of others. That makes success less a possession to be protected, and means that in any success I have I am the figurehead or spokesperson of the success of others. It also means that when failure happens, as inevitably it does, I don't have to carry that myself either.

When I did the triple triathlon challenge for Sport Relief back in 2020 it was, of course, tough. Three triathlons in three days in three cities, but the hard part wasn't the actual running, cycling and swimming, the hardest part for me was accepting that I wasn't going to win. My success at the event wouldn't be in crossing the finish line first, that wasn't going to happen. Rather my success would be in accepting that I was going to be last. When it was all over there was a party and the physio, an ex-army officer built like a brick privy, nicknamed 'Dot', came over and said, 'You were my little superstar, you never lost heart.' Truth is, the only reason I crossed the finish line at all was because him and the rest of the huge team dragged me over it. Don't get me wrong, they couldn't run the steps for me, but they did everything but. Every success is never individually won.

It's not about the money

The Bible is often misquoted or taken out of context. Perhaps one of the most well-known and yet misquoted lines is 'Money is the root of all evil' – the actual quote is 'The *love* of money is the root of all evil.' The word 'love' makes a crucial difference to me – it's not about the money, it's about how we act with it.

Should we value money and material abundance? Does it make us bad people to want nice things around us and pursue a state of wealth? You probably think I think money and the love of it is a terrible thing. And you'd be right, I do think it's bad to want or pursue those things at the expense of other people. But like it or not, money is essential for us to survive in this world. The noble idea that money doesn't buy you happiness is all very nice, but it's usually only wealthy people who say it. Having grown up without much money, the idea of living a good, honest life without any cash to spare is actually the opposite of what I believe. As my dad used to say, 'Money might not be able to buy you happiness, but it can buy you a better class of misery.' And when you've experienced that first-hand you learn its importance, but that doesn't mean it should be valued before all else.

Human beings aren't very good with things they can't see and touch and taste. Being the creatures that we are, controlled by our senses, we like stuff we can point to. Did well in your swimming lesson? You'll need a certificate. Got a promotion? You get a pay rise! Which of course means a bigger car or a better house or a flashier label on your trainers. Money and possessions have long been an indicator of success. Social gatherings are a great way to demonstrate to the rest of the community just how financially successful you are. Wander round any graveyard, especially the Victorian ones, and it's easy to spot who were the mill workers and who were the mill owners.

But having witnessed my fair share of success stories, I've learned that financial success comes with its own fallout. I once did a wedding for the daughter of a scrap dealer. He'd made a fortune selling scrap iron and despite his own humble beginnings he'd sent his kids to the best private school and given them all the opportunities he felt he'd never had. While he spoke with a broad Essex twang, they had cut-glass vowels. While he still lifted scrap on to his truck every day, his daughter wore a wedding dress the price of a small car as he walked her up the aisle. It was a lovely ceremony with a packed church and I know everyone enjoyed it, but I'll never forget the way he looked in his morning suit. I've never seen a suit look so uncomfortable. And not because it didn't fit him but because he didn't fit it. At one point later in the day he leant over and whispered in my ear that he didn't know anyone there. He was an alien at his own daughter's wedding. Was he a success? Call it success or simply earning lots of money, either way it had rendered him a little bit lost.

This isn't just something I've observed in others either – my own career and the path it has taken has taught me that what might externally look like success doesn't necessarily mean you feel successful. I was a secondary school teacher long before I became a priest. I always knew I wanted a job where people looked at me – a rebellion against the idea that you shouldn't draw attention to yourself? Perhaps. Ironically, it was my mum who started it all, though. She was a school cleaner, and in the holidays she signed me up for a Shakespeare drama club that took place in the school where she worked, so that she could keep a bit of an eye on me while she was at work. I think she also knew just how much I'd love it. I particularly loved Meg Jepson, the teacher. She was adamant that Shakespeare was for everybody and it didn't matter what your background was. So at eleven years old I found myself workshopping Ariel from *The Tempest*.

Meg would insist we cleaned the workspace before our day started, teaching us discipline and respect. There was an eclectic mix of children, teenagers and young adults. The framework Meg had for the group was 'no special friendships', so I learned to talk and get along with everyone. There was also an expectation that rather than just learn your own lines for the play you would learn everyone else's too, so that at a moment's notice you could step in if needed.

I didn't know this wasn't the way all youth theatres were run and so I diligently learned the whole of the play off by heart. It stood me in good stead, especially on the night Meg decided to change the casting last-minute and I found myself playing a part I hadn't rehearsed. There was no sneaking off to the dressing-room when you weren't on, either. The cast who weren't on stage would stand in the wings listening to the performance and supporting everyone else. I loved my youth theatre days, so when it came to thinking about my future career, teaching seemed like a guaranteed way to incorporate having some kind of audience into my working day, even if the audience was sullen teenagers, uninterested in learning about religion in RE.

I originally thought I'd be a primary school teacher but once I realized you had to teach maths – the Devil's own subject – I decided to go for secondary. I went for theology because I knew that no one liked RE and therefore, if I could go in there and make them laugh and get them to enjoy the lessons, I stood a better chance of being the best teacher they'd ever had. I like approval. You might have thought that I'd grown up in a religious family to make that decision so early on in life, but no – it was all about finding the easiest route to applause. Funny how a whole career can hang off such seemingly unimportant choices.

I was christened as a baby, like many of us were in the 1970s, but we never went to church as a family. Religion always fascinated me though, even as a child. I remember I got a book token for my eighth birthday from my uncle Edward and spent it on an illustrated New

Testament. That was how I rolled. Later on, at secondary school, I was invited to church by my mate Katie (who I'm still the best of friends with and who is godmother to my youngest), which led me to become a member of the Christian Union; I had been moved up to top set in my class, due to my uncommon appetite for learning, and in an attempt to make friends with the nice girls in my new set, I joined them at CU and church.

Without my school Christian Union and the church youth group, I might never have found my faith. But I often cringe now at the thought of its fundamental, evangelical nature. Christian Union at my school was a well-meaning group who took it upon themselves, in the enthusiasm of youth, to evangelize kids (and sometimes teachers) in the corridors. We would meet on Wednesday lunchtimes and discuss sin, while most of our fellow classmates were having a wonderful time smoking fags round the PE block – actually doing some sinning. We took it all very seriously. I remember a long-drawn-out conversation around the movie *Ghost* and whether it was OK to go and see it because it involved clairvoyance, a practice more commonly associated with paganism than Christianity. I never said Christian Union was logical. We also talked a lot about what was acceptable to do if you got a boyfriend (he would naturally be Christian, because the thought of dating anyone who didn't believe in Jesus was inconceivable). The consensus was that if you did anything beyond holding hands you would be on very dodgy spiritual ground. We had talks from pro-life speakers and I remember being genuinely frightened that unless I got my mum and dad to 'give their life to Jesus' and pray a special prayer, they were definitely going to be damned for all eternity and it would probably be all my fault.

In many ways it was an easier way to have faith – you were either saved or not, in or out, going to heaven or hell with clearly defined boundaries. I'm as certain in my faith now as ever, but my faith and what it means to me is not as simplistic. I've grown up. I don't think evangelicals, or even Christians, have a monopoly on faith. And I look back on some of the things I believed then and I feel uncomfortable. But I smile too, though, at fifteen-year-old Me's naivety about the world.

When I announced that I wanted to study theology, and at a Catholic college of all places, the people at church and some of my friends at Christian Union wondered how on earth I would be able to teach other faiths? The parent of one friend expressed concern that in understanding other faiths and in studying my own, I would gain too much 'head knowledge' and not enough 'heart knowledge'. That by studying theology I was putting my own salvation in danger. A fear that asking too many questions would lead to doubt and uncertainty, which in the Christian tradition I found myself in at that point were very much the enemy. As it turns out, I only went to the Christian Union at university twice and then gave up on it (bowling and polite pizza could not compete with rugby, boys and beer), but that didn't mean my faith wavered. In fact, doubt and uncertainty were and still are my best friends, their external pressure causing my faith, like a diamond, to become more valuable and beautiful.

Still, it was the path I had my heart set on and, once I'd made it, I absolutely loved being a secondary school teacher. I did my teaching practice at a wide range of schools. Both a posh fee-paying girls' school and a school on the estate in Bradford where they filmed the 80s comedy drama *Rita, Sue and Bob Too* (which hopefully at least some of you remember). It was there that I had chairs thrown at me and a kid show me his knife. I also worked at a standard local comprehensive close to where my own parents had grown up forty years before. It was a bit rough around the edges, but never dull. The kind of school where it was no surprise to see a dog casually wandering along the corridor in break times. One of the kids' dads was a lollipop man, or rather he was doing community service as a lollipop man. One morning, as parents were bringing their kids into school, a car clipped him and so he smashed the back windscreen in with his lollipop. Later that day his son stole a digger and drove it around the school car park – though I'm still unsure as to whether the two events were related. A few months later the same lad heard I was struggling to sell my car, so he offered to nick and torch it for me for the insurance. He was bewildered when I declined.

Perhaps predictably, I hated all the planning and admin of being a teacher, but I really loved teaching.

And I was good at it! I know that I made lessons fun for those kids. When it was time to talk about Nativity, I got my mate to bring her baby in so the children could see what Jesus might have looked like. When it was Eid, I brought food in and we had a feast. When it was Diwali, we'd have a go at some dancing. I did a whole scheme of work on the spirituality of *The Simpsons* and all the different faiths that are represented – this was when kids still watched broadcast television. We'd have a go at it all.

There were a lot of kids there who didn't know what success felt like, who never got the gold stars or the headteacher's awards. It was before the dreaded Ofsted had really taken hold of the RE curriculum, so I was still relatively free to teach how and what I wanted. As a result I was given the graveyard slot: double RE on a Friday afternoon, and you can imagine how engaged every student was by then. Still, it meant I could teach how I wanted to. I remain extremely proud of the fact that in one of these classes I taught a bunch of the less academically gifted kids, mostly boys, how to make balloon animals, a couple of magic tricks and how to juggle. I wanted them to leave my class feeling like they could do something that no one else in that school could. Even if they were making cock-and-balls balloon models when I turned my back, when they finished my class I knew they could go into any room and bring complete joy to whoever was there by making a sausage dog balloon model. Success? To me and to them, yes. To Ofsted, less so.

Success changes

So I had a good job, teaching a subject I loved, and felt like I'd ticked the 'success' box set out by society. But it was spending time at home after having my children that made me realize that my calling – my own version of success – lay elsewhere. I was a relatively young mum – just twenty-three when I married and twenty-five when Ruby was born (Arthur came along two years later) – and it soon became apparent, because of just how knackering it is to raise small humans, that going back to teaching in any meaningful sense was going to have to happen in the far-off distant future, if it happened at all.

I don't mind admitting that I didn't always love being at home with small children. I used to get us all out of the house in the morning and not go back until dinner time, just to avoid the mess and the endless cleaning up after children. It really made me question the point of 'me'. What was I for? I realize now it's a question lots of mums at home with young children ask themselves. A successful day when you've got babies and toddlers is mostly about survival. You win a series of tiny, almost invisible victories all day – a good feed, a routine stuck to, a basket of laundry washed – and there is no one there to see it, or to say well done.

I was restless at home, and I knew I needed something else to do; despite being an absolute boss at playdough I was short-tempered when it came to tolerating the snail trail of toddler snot that permanently stained my shoulder. I wanted to be useful – or at least more useful than I felt I was at the time. I knew that the church we were part of wanted a warden, so I took that on as a voluntary post. Contrary to what you might expect, given my current position writing this book as an ecclesiastical expert, I was the worst churchwarden there's ever been. Not only because I was fantastically uninterested in all the tasks I was meant to carry out as a churchwarden, but because I found I was always chatting to the parishioners and popping in on people and generally being an accidental vicar. Churchwardens are supposed to concern themselves with fire extinguishers and lightning conductors, but I couldn't even fake interest in those. I did get a kick out of having powers of arrest, though. (In England, churchwardens have special powers of arrest that allow them to keep the peace in churchyards. I was hoping I'd have to break up a few boozy parties or even some light hanky-panky, but alas, I never got the chance.)

I was already the 'religious one' in my family because of my teaching job, and people tended to come to me for all their religious needs – would I do the prayers at my cousin's wedding, or say Grace at Christmas dinner – so taking on this role felt like a natural thing for me. I remember telling my friend Denise that I felt this deep need to nourish and feed people – physically and metaphorically (I still always carry snacks). I thought that becoming a warden would just mean being one of the people to help at communion, when we have the bread and wine at church, but it turned out to be the first seed of a call to priesthood, what we call a vocation.

Doing it on purpose

'Find out who you are and do it on purpose.' The immortal words of Dolly Parton are as true today as ever. As I got older, being successful began to look less like detached houses and sunshine holidays, or even a degree and a good job, and more like being true to myself. And, as I came to realize, that sometimes means being brave enough to take steps in a new direction.

The decision to become a vicar was not one I took lightly. Friends had often suggested to me that getting ordained was something I should think about, but I'd never really taken it seriously. I suspect this was because I saw being a vicar as something for other people. Vicars were men, they were middle-class, they had nicer accents. I didn't take it seriously because I thought it would be about me 'showing off' and attention-seeking, something which in the holy world of the church is surely a deplorable trait. It was so far from my own family's story, and from being a mum, which felt like my whole identity now that I'd finished working as a teacher.

I had been serving as a churchwarden for about two years and in that time I had also become a vicar's personal assistant. As well as giving me valuable insight into what the job of a priest might be, being a warden and a

PA meant I had to work really closely with my boss, so it wasn't unusual for us to spend time together. I did find it a bit odd, though, when he invited me out for dinner one night, just the two of us. Was he going to make an indecent proposal? No, it was much worse and infinitely more shocking. He took me out for a curry and somewhere between the poppadums and the tikka masala, quietly suggested I should look into the possibility of ordination. It was only then that it began to seem like a possibility; when your vicar tips you the wink like that, you need to do something about it. When God offers you a job – you don't turn it down.

And so began the process of discernment. In the Church of England, this is a long and often complicated period in which potential new vicars are assessed and evaluated for their suitability, before going ahead with their full training. Kind of like those old *Police Academy* films, except that instead of our fitness or our capacity for fighting crime, we are 'discerned' on such qualities as our wisdom, our love of God and our capacity for 'fruitfulness' (which roughly translated means an ability to tolerate other people's nonsense). The process is tailored to the individual and as such is different for everyone. For some people it can take years, for others a few months, but for everyone it involves essays and interviews, work experience and prayer. So. Much. Prayer.

It also meant being sent along on placements to have a look at how other churches do what they do. Every church thinks that the way they 'do church' is the normal way of doing things. But as someone who's been to lots of different churches, I know that each one has a slightly different way of doing what they do. Apart from my time at university, when I worshipped as a Roman Catholic, most of my church experience in my teenage years and when I was newly married was in the evangelical charismatic tradition. A tradition that is sometimes called 'happy clappy'. Preaching was really important, and my church didn't really wear robes or do much liturgy (liturgy is the set words that the service is supposed to follow). So during my discernment process for ministry I was sent off to a much higher church than mine in a much more multicultural area of Sheffield. The church I was sent to used incense (the sweet-smelling perfume that is burnt as part of worship to make an aroma pleasing to God, although it does also rather usefully mask any pungent odours any members of the congregation with questionable hygiene might have), had communion (the bread and wine eaten to remember Jesus) with everything, and the music was led by a choir and an organ, not by guitars and keyboards like I was used to. They also said morning and evening prayer every day, using the set words. Before I went there I didn't even know that the Church of England had set prayers for every day. It was also the first place where I ever wore robes to preach, and the first time I would experience a problem that has followed me to every church I've ever been to since. I'm very short, and the robes most churches keep in their vestry cupboards are not made for people who are shorter than Kylie. (For the record, I am officially shorter than Kylie. I've met her twice, and the first time we stood back to back to check.) I've tripped up many a chancel step (the raised bit around the altar) in my time. I'm pleased to say that when I've preached at Westminster Abbey and St Paul's they've had an extensive wardrobe catering for everyone, though more rural parish churches don't have the same resources, so I've taken to always having a pocketful of safety pins and impossibly high heels with me, which usually solves the problem.

I'll never forget getting the call to say I'd passed the selection process. It had been an exhausting couple of years, concluding with a kind of *X Factor* Judges' Houses for vicars where I found myself playing croquet in a country house with other wannabe priests. Outside my comfort zone doesn't really cover it. When I got the call we were in the park and I'd just taken Arthur to the hideous public loo there. He had just done a big poo when the phone rang, and as I picked up the phone to answer it I shouted, 'Arthur, don't touch it with your fingers!' It seems that the discernment process somehow set the tone, as my life hasn't become any less bizarre since. I have lost count of how many time I've thought, 'How the hell did I get here?' A particularly memorable one was recording a Christmas edition of *The Wheel*, sandwiched between Christopher Biggins and Clare Balding as we spun round like we were on a fairground waltzer. Clare nearly came a cropper on that one, by the way – her chair experienced a minor malfunction and at one point seemed to start gently smoking. Thankfully they didn't waste any time sorting her out; the woman's a national treasure.

Me becoming a priest meant my husband, Graham (though I imagine many of you already knew that), had to leave his job as a music teacher so that we could move closer to the college (or vicar school) and I could finish my training. I remember at the time someone asked me which college I would go to. I chose Nottingham because it was the one nearest my family and meant I could easily get home to Sheffield to see them, and that seemed to me to make the most sense. Although Graham and the children moved with me for my training and we rented a house, my lovely mum was very poorly at the time and spent months in hospital following a heart attack and complications. So I drove back to Sheffield two or three times a week to visit her and support my dad. I was still fantastically unaware of and naive about the code that exists, even in the clergy, about where you receive your education and what it says about you and your place in the world. I didn't realize that that person's question about which college I'd go to had been loaded, and by choosing a college that wasn't Durham or Oxbridge I had already scuppered any chances of promotion in the church. And that the college I had chosen said something about what particular tribe within the church I belonged to. It's a code rooted in the class system which is as old as the concept of education itself. I'm still learning the code, although sometimes I find that my naivety is actually an asset; it means that often I have more confidence going into a conversation than I should have. I've learned that the question, 'And where did you train?' is about so much more than the awarding body of your degree, it can define your future successes and mean that the person asking the question will assume a lot about your views based on your answer. There are all sorts of subtle messages like these in this profession that I had no awareness about, such as how many buttons you have on your cassock: apparently more buttons means you are more likely to be from a higher, more catholic church tradition, fewer buttons means a lower church tradition, less smells and bells. I didn't know this, I just picked the cassock that wasn't dry clean only.

Was it a successful move, to leave teaching and uproot my family? I think so. I'm certainly happy, which in turn means they mostly are. It was successful in so far as I did what I set out to: get ordained, be a vicar. But who's to say if I hadn't done that I wouldn't have found success as a teacher? And later on, when the flash mob I oversaw at a wedding went viral, and the whole world weighed in with its opinions on whether or not I was fit to be a vicar and what women like me were doing to the church, was that success or a failure? As I write this I don't technically have a congregation of my own, I'm more of a priestly nomad, combining my work in telly and radio with being a supply vicar. Giant success or epic fail? Who can say? Ultimately, success means something

different to everyone, according to their own circumstances and expectations. And the truth is, I'm as beguiled
by it all as everyone else.

Start with the end

So although it might be what our minds first go to, I
don't think anyone really thinks success is about money
and status, do they? I don't think anyone really thinks
it's about power, either. I used to think success was
making my mum and dad proud; being the first one
in the family to go to university felt like success. But
these days, having had a variety of jobs, children and
other big life events, I think success is hard to put your
finger on at the present moment, it's much easier to
reflect on. And I've found that the real test of success
is what people say about you when you're not around
any more.

As a vicar I am privileged to be a guest at the funerals of many people, a large proportion of whom I've
never met. It might sound like a gloomy task, but very
often funerals are joyful and life-affirming occasions
and I can honestly say they are a favourite part of my
job. I also think it's really important, once in a while, to
be confronted by and to consider our own mortality,
and funerals do that so beautifully. Of course, they are
also extremely sad, and rightly so. But for me the sad-
dest funerals are not those of children or people who

have left us in tragic circumstances, or before their time – although they are of course both heartbreaking and distressing. For me, the worst funerals are those when there is nothing to say about the person we are sending off.

There is truly nothing sadder for me than meeting the family of the person I am about to send off to the 'what comes next' and asking them about their relative, only to find they don't have very much to say about them. They didn't see enough of them, or they lost touch. They don't know if they had any hobbies or who their friends were. They hadn't seen them for years. Or have nothing to say because the person who has died never seemed to do very much. That's not me judging anyone's lifestyle choice, perhaps they were content with a life of *Countdown* and custard creams, perhaps for them that was success, but perhaps it wasn't. Sometimes I have to leave large silences in the service, to allow things that were unsaid to be heard silently, but also sometimes just to fill the time.

In those moments it strikes me that perhaps a measurement of true success is living a life that, when the time comes, provides ample material for your eulogy, the speech delivered by the minister at a funeral. Have you ever wondered what people will say at your funeral? Just have a think about it now for a second: what will your eulogy say?

I'll tell you three things we vicars never talk about in eulogies: how much someone weighed ('and then in her thirties, Sarah lost three stone with Weight Watchers and was able to finally wear that bikini' somehow just never crops up); how rich they were ('and then Richard qualified for a Gold Amex card and his life changed forever' also never gets said); and how clean a person's house was ('you could eat your dinner off Linda's skirting boards' is also definitely not something I've ever heard), so it is completely pointless to waste any time thinking about these things. You're welcome.

I've also been at a few bedsides of people who are coming to the end of their life. Part of my job in those rooms is to facilitate the conversation around death and dying. I usually ask to speak to the person alone. And the dying have shared some wisdom with me over the years. They usually say that their life has been good, that they've tried their best, and when we talk about the good things, the successes if you like, they talk about family and friends, the relationships they were part of in terms of their community. They talk about the things they enjoyed: gardening, their job, dancing, and they talk about what mattered to them, their values, being truthful or hardworking. Success to the dying is measured by love, who they loved, what they loved and how they loved.

And when the time comes to write their eulogy, I write from those themes too. Success is not about how educated you are or how far from your own upbringing you have travelled, certainly not about how 'holy' you've been. I think it's about measuring connection with others. It's about having something of your own, a story, and something you believed in, a value you had, the love that you shared.

THREE GOOD THINGS

When you're pondering your own successes in life and wondering what it's all about, these three things will help you recognize your own triumphs and bolster the spirits of others:

1. **Take a moment to look down the mountain.**

   Sometimes we are so focused on where we are going and what's coming next that it's easy to forget just how far we have come. Take the time to take stock. This could mean simply looking back over old photos or writing a list of some of the things you've done and been through. It can mean calling an old friend to reminisce about something you went through together, or celebrating seemingly mundane successes. You got your baby to sleep through the night, you ticked off all the things on your to-do list, you remembered an aunt's birthday and got the card in the post on time. These seemingly innocuous things might mean very little to others, but acknowledging them to yourself sets your mind on the right path. You can look back over the past year, the past week or just reflect on your day – the point is that you reflect, and remind yourself of how far you have come. Celebrate the mundane successes. Rejoice in them and allow yourself to feel pleased. Write your eulogy.

2. **Gather your cheerleaders.**

Surround yourself with the people who want to celebrate you, who lift you up and make you feel good about yourself. People who say, 'Go you!' My daughter Ruby is my biggest cheerleader. A few years ago I took part in a challenge for Sport Relief: I somehow signed up for 'Dare to Tri' as a challenge that involved completing three triathlons in three cities over three days. When I signed up for it I realized that the last time I rode a bike it had stabilizers. Graham couldn't believe I'd said yes. The training was extremely demanding, and every day, Ruby sent me a video of Michelle Obama sending an open message to Beyoncé, about how amazing she is. If you've never seen it, I urge you to have a Google and behold the pure love and appreciation that flows from Michelle to Queen B, one woman to another. Gather your cheerleaders, the people who make you feel six feet tall (I'm five feet and even just an extra four inches would be lovely). And remember to be somebody else's cheerleader too – because that shit is precious.

3. **Work on your jealousy.**

We all feel jealous of other people's successes, it's natural. The trick is not to pretend it never happens, but to approach it with curiosity. When a colleague gets a promotion, try to bury your jealous feelings and instead ask yourself why you're feeling this way. I love the phrase (and it will crop up a few times in the book), 'It's never about what it's about.' What does your jealousy tell you about yourself? Do you wish you had tried harder for the job? Then how can you do things differently next time? Or maybe you need a whole new job? Let the jealousy be a mirror to your real feelings and take a good look!

2. Love

You might think that love happens at first sight, or grows over time. Perhaps you think love is a feeling that we don't have control over, something that happens to us, like being struck by lightning, or catching a cold. The truth is, I think love is more a decision, and a decision that we have to keep making.

You probably think that I think true, godly love means no sex before marriage, getting married in a church and staying married to the same person forever. You might also imagine that, being a vicar, I'm against gay love, trans love, divorce and every other kind of love that deviates from the path of what some might call 'right-eousness'. There was a time when perhaps all that was mostly true, back when I was a teenager monitoring the corridors for any unholy touching, but I'm much older now and wiser, and I've theologically grown up. My life experience has informed my understanding and I know that love is expressed in a myriad of more complicated and beautiful ways.

For a lot of folk, being in love means getting married, so it will come as no surprise that I will talk a fair bit in this chapter about my experience of doing weddings. However, I'm very much aware that marriage isn't for

everyone, and for some people it's not as straightforward as that. Despite changes in the law allowing
same-sex couples to marry, the Church of England,
along with other faith groups, is exempt from some of
those laws, and so does not yet offer marriage services
for anyone other than heterosexual couples. There's lots
of us feeling very cross about this, lots of us trying to
campaign to get it changed, and lots of us asking serious
questions about if we can stay in a church that continues
with this stance. Recent changes have seen the introduc-
tion of some prayers that we can say with same-sex
couples after they have had a civil marriage outside the
church building. It's a step in the right direction but
there's still a long way to go.

Until the Marriage Act of 1753, marriage in England,
much like elsewhere in Europe, was a purely civic affair,
a purely private partnership that no official body had any
business in; no ceremony or witnesses were needed, but
as a result of the changes to the law the formalization of
a relationship became the responsibility of vicars and
the like, who were kind of seen as the experts on getting
wed. But that is rapidly changing. With the changes to
the Marriage Act (1994), which incidentally was introduced as a private member's bill by Gyles Brandreth (yes,
that Gyles Brandreth), it meant your choice of venue for
the big day was not limited to a registry office or a church.
You could now get married in castles, hotels and stately
homes. This change in culture means that often people
will now prefer to have a quiet legal ceremony at the

registry office and then a 'what looks like a wedding but legally isn't' at a venue of their choice with a celebrant. While I'm sad, of course, that the church is doing fewer weddings, I do rejoice at the creativity that the changes in law and culture have brought about. One thing remains the same, though: whether it's church, castle or hotel there seems to be a human need for ritual to mark our love for one another and that we still believe in monogamy for life. And for so many it feels like church is the proper place for that, or at least having hymns and a blessing. Weddings outside of church are no less weddings, of course, but tradition matters to many, and churches somehow provide that effortlessly and with a different quality to perhaps more corporate venues.

The rules around civil weddings are pretty strict, the main distinction being that you aren't allowed any mention of faith or belief and you have to have a registrar. This leads many couples to go for the option of having a legal ceremony first, separate from the ceremony they invite their family and friends to. Strictly speaking the wedding is when the legal contract is formalized, but, in reality, if that bit is done quietly and on a wet Wednesday afternoon in the town registry office and subsequently there's a ceremony which has no legal clout but all the emotional bits, it's safe to say it's obvious which one most people will consider the 'real' wedding.

Often when we meet couples wanting to be married in church there's an awkwardness. They aren't sure what they believe, they haven't been to church since school and they are expecting a negative response from a judge-mental vicar, and that's if they get as far as making the phone call or sending the email. I know the church hasn't always been great at giving a generous welcome to those who want to get married there. I know loads of vicars who are welcoming and generous with their time, but sadly some old-school church folk can get a bit sniffy about couples with no connection to church using it as a venue for their big day, in the same way as they might book the flowers or the cars. But I don't mind so much. I'm glad we are still being used. There are so many other pretty options out there, venues that would be only too happy to take your money and be much nicer than some churches are about it, so I'm chuffed to bits to see couples wanting to be married in church. Maybe they don't come again for years, or ever, but if getting married in church allows them to celebrate the tiny speck of faith they might have, and it makes their special day more special, why should we begrudge them that?

Take it to church

When I finished my curacy and started in my first parishes, one of the churches I looked after was a huge priory church. It was built within living memory of the Norman conquests and was originally a place for naughty Benedictine monks to be exiled and punished for their misdemeanours. It was a great barn of a building, able to seat hundreds in a village that would never fill it. The finances weren't great and the contact with anyone younger than fifty years old in the community was largely limited to school assemblies. So when I started there, I looked around to see what else was going on in the community and how the church might be able to get involved. Just up the road was a country estate – the house and gardens had been in the same family for generations, but like a lot of English stately homes it had needed to diversify and adapt to survive. They were a licensed venue and open for weddings. One of my first weekends in post I took myself off to the wedding fayre that was happening at the house to see if we might think about working together. The house and the church were just off the A1, so it was a great location for lots of couples. Being so accessible also meant that people who weren't local had receptions there too.

Now, before I go any further with this story, there are some very complicated rules about who can and can't be married in a Church of England church. The idea is that people should get married in their parish or local church, or a church where they have a special connection, like if their parents were married there or it's where they were baptized. If a bride and groom have no special connection to the parish church they want to get married in, they are legally obliged to form a connection by attending the church for a period of six months. I love this process, because it means we at the church (the 'church family' as I call us) get to be part of the preparations.

Being part of the build-up means that we can all get excited about the big day in the run-up to it. In fact, in a rural church with a largely elderly congregation a bride and groom can sometimes become sort of temporary grandchildren.

Back to the story . . . As far as I could see, hooking up with our local wedding venue and helping more couples to get married in our beautiful priory church was a win for everyone involved: the wedding reception venue got to offer the parish church as another option for the ceremony bit of the day, I got to be part of a wonderful day of celebrating love and talking about God, and my treasurer could see me earning my keep. (People at weddings are usually in a good mood, happy to be in church, willing to put something in the collection, and, if they've had a quick pint in the pub beforehand, they'll also join in with the hymns. Happy days!) Before I started at that church there were about six weddings a year; by the time I left we were regularly holding twenty. I was really proud of that. It wasn't just a numbers game, though. I wanted the couples getting married in the priory church I took care of to have the best wedding. One guest said to me on the way out of the church, 'I thought the reception would be the best bit, but I really enjoyed that.' That moment of praise really stuck with me. What would it be like if I was able to surprise people at weddings with how much they 'enjoyed' the service? Now that's not to say I see the ceremony as entertainment or its sole purpose to be enjoyable, it's not always about that. But I think it does have something to do with hospitality. The whole of the marriage service is about love, the love of two people for one another, the love of their families and friends, and in a church wedding the love of God. How might I communicate some of that love? Well, I think a good way is by being hospitable: after the ceremony the guests leaving won't shake the vicar's hand and say, 'I felt loved,' but they will say words like 'I enjoyed that,' or 'That was a lovely service.' I wanted people to have a good time at weddings, to think of church as a place of love, welcome and joy. My role as the person at the front is to host that. And, when it comes to the couple getting married, if their friends and family have a good time, they might feel loved too. But I also wanted them to be able to personalize their service. Church of England weddings are often assumed to be the safe, traditional option. There are some bits of the service that can't be changed: the vows, for example, are the same for everyone. But the choice of music, or readings, or any extras can all be adapted and personalized. And it's because of one of those extras, and because of love, that I ended up on television.

Gary and Tracey had been engaged for nine years, so their big day had been a while coming. Gary had been married before, but this was Tracey's first time and they both wanted to do things 'properly'. They didn't have any connection to my church, but they were having the reception locally and so this church made sense. I went about setting up regular meetings to make sure that within the legalities of the Church of England, Gary and Tracey were able to get married in the parish church on my watch. Happily, this meant we had plenty of time to get to know each other in the run-up to the wedding. Tracey sang in a musical theatre choir and, like me, was a bit of a performer. When a couple of extroverts get together it's natural for them to bounce off each other. To this day, they will tell you that the flash mob we all did that day was my idea, but I'm sure it was theirs, although I do confess that I had always fancied doing one. And even though by this stage flash mobs were already very dated, the Church of England is always a healthy twenty years behind any trend!

A flash mob was perfect for Gary and Tracey, and for their guests, but I've also married plenty of couples for whom this sort of thing would have been a nightmare. One size doesn't fit all. In my job I'm sometimes asked how I stop myself crying at the emotional bits; after all, so much of what I find myself involved in are the big parts of people's lives – the happy and the sad. The answer is you remain professional, there's a job to be done so you get on with it and do it. But there have been times when even in the depths of my professionalism I've wobbled. One of those times was when a particularly shy couple came to get married. They wanted to keep things really simple. They just had their parents as witnesses, no guests, no flowers, no hymns, just a simple service with her in a nice frock and him in a tie. It's a mistake to think that a church wedding means a big wedding – it doesn't have to. But their wedding, with none of the literal bells and metaphorical whistles, was no less of a ceremony. Their love for each other and the love of those around them was not diminished because the flowers didn't cost the price of a holiday. They chose to express their love for one another in a simpler way, but an expression of love it still was. A flash mob wouldn't have been right for them, but it was right for Gary and Tracey. Love is love but it is often expressed and demonstrated in many different ways, and those ways reflect the person expressing the love and the person receiving it.

Whoever's idea the flash mob was, once they'd decided they were going to do it, Gary and Tracey took it very seriously and had nine weeks of wedding rehearsals, which with hindsight I wish I'd also taken more seriously. If I'd known they were going to post it on YouTube and it would get around 10 million hits around the globe, I might have practised a bit more. I would certainly have worn a better bra. Nevertheless, the video of the congregation throwing our best shapes to the dance music anthem 'Everybody Dance Now', segued with Kool and the Gang's 'Celebrate (good times)' in church, was spotted by a producer at Channel 4 and the rest, as they say, is history.

I remember the *Gogglebox* phone call like it was yesterday. It came the same week as a call from a producer from the UK version of *Married at First Sight*. Programme-makers were looking for a spiritual consultant for the show to appear on camera (an idea they dropped after the first two series). This sounded like a good idea to me on paper (after all, other cultures different from mine have been doing guided marriages for centuries), but I knew that it would be really controversial for a vicar to appear there. A friend took up their invitation instead and got himself into hot water for it, undeservedly I thought. But *Gogglebox* we said yes to almost straight away. Graham was a fan of the first series, which had been shown in the wee small hours on Channel 4, so it was a no-brainer. The *Gogglebox* team came to the vicarage and gave us a sort of audition to see if the dynamic would work. Hilariously, they didn't really want me to be partnered with Graham, instead they were looking for me to sit alongside a female friend in order to channel a *Vicar of Dibley* vibe. But Graham was my natural telly-watching chum, so it seemed weird for it not to be him. The show was edited to make it look like he hardly spoke, which I felt fostered a somewhat misogynistic narrative of me as the bossy woman and Graham as the hen-pecked husband. The truth is Graham says loads, he just talks in massively long sentences and mumbles, so it was difficult to edit him into the punchy eight-second clips that work on *Gogglebox*.

I'll always have such fond memories of that crazy wedding day that launched us on to reality TV – and I'm pleased to report that Gary and Tracey are still grooving away happily together. The video of the flash mob has become the central bit of my material for my after-dinner speaking. I watch it now in halls full of WI members who don't know what's coming next, and to hear the spontaneous laughter as the dance starts and the gasp of delight as others join in never fails to make me happy. I still love it. There were plenty who didn't love the clip at the time and were very vocal about it. I stopped reading the comments under the original video pretty quickly. The crux of most of the complaints, once I'd sifted through the inevitable anti-women priests nonsense, was that somehow I didn't take my faith or my vocation seriously. Because I was dancing in church. The nay-sayers seemed to miss the point: it was only because I am serious about my faith that I did the dance in the first place. There's much to argue about in religion and philosophy, but it seems to me that one of the few things that is a bedrock of every expression of spirituality is the central importance of love. And that when love is seen it should be named, celebrated and nurtured in any and every way possible. Church should always be a place of welcome; no one within its walls is perfect but in glorious imperfection lies its beauty. Sadly the lack of warmth and welcome by some has meant that visitors to services don't stay very long or come back again at all. And we all know one hard-nosed, ungracious opinion can undo a multitude of kindness.

Unfortunately, not everything at weddings is about love, though. With the desire for a day to be the perfect expression of a couple's love for one another comes an inevitable shadow which usually manifests as jealousy and competitiveness. The need to outdo others' outfits, locations, food, music . . . the list goes on. This path can be perilous. Of course, it's every couple's aim to make it the best day possible for them and their guests, and that's been the case for centuries, but often this can get in the way of what's important. There is often so much focus around the wedding day itself, but not always on what lies ahead. There's always so much chat about dresses and flowers, venues and rings and, if you are Gary and Tracey, when to put your hands in the air, but less chat about what happens after that. People seem to forget that love lives, it's like a living, breathing thing that needs to be fed and nurtured. It can't go uncared for and untended. It grows, changes, blossoms, but it can also wither and die. The job of the couple once they've made those promises is to figure out how they are going to keep them, how their unique love for one another will continue to thrive.

To support this process when I was in parish I used to hold a 'couples' day' for all the people I was going to be marrying in the next year or so. A traditional church wedding day can be a bit of a marathon, so I'd get together all the couples that were going to be married and we'd have a little run-through of the vows, do any legal stuff that needed doing, and introduce them to the organist and the florists and any other people they needed to know.

Most couples getting married are in their twenties or thirties, so, with an expectation, and hope, that they'll live into their eighties or nineties, most couples are looking at the next fifty or sixty years together. I like to throw that into the conversation, when they are wondering whether to have pink flowers or yellow ones, and whether to sing 'Jerusalem' or 'Morning Has Broken'. Potentially sixty years of waking up next to that person. Sixty years of their habits and foibles. Sixty years of health, wealth and happiness, or perhaps the opposite. You'd think this wouldn't be a surprise to anyone, but more often than not there are couples looking back at me with a look of stark realization on their faces. The focus up to now has been on how they will make it to the wedding day with so much to organize, and then how to make it through the day itself. In the same way that people expecting a baby don't stop to think about what parenting teens might be like, no bride is really thinking about what he's going to look like at eighty. So I always remind couples on their wedding day that they won't always look this good, or be in such good health, to bring home what they already know and hope, that this isn't just about the day, this is for life.

The wedding vows we say in church back me up, of course. I think they are crafted the way they are for good reason. At the core of the vows is the idea of good times and bad, sickness and health – this isn't a sugar-coated Disney fairy-tale, this is an honest declaration that it isn't going to be all plain sailing. It's a sobering moment when the realization hits, that this could be it for the next sixty years. It's why, incidentally, couples can choose to say something extra to each other as they take their vows, but the church doesn't allow the core vows to be changed or altered. The vows are the manifesto for the marriage, the guidelines for how the love that seems so over-whelming on the wedding day might still be alive in many years to come. When you're standing there in a crisp white wedding dress, the wedding vows ask you to con-sider what it might be like to have to wipe the other person's arse one day when they can no longer do it themselves, so I like to remind them of that fact before they have a captive audience.

I've never had anyone back out, but I have had a few couples that have been taken aback at the thought, usu-ally at the preparation day and rehearsals. They all want to rise to the challenge, though. No one walks down the aisle thinking they are going to get divorced, or if they do they don't vocalize it. But I think it's probably also true that no one walks down the aisle really considering how long they might be in this for. I certainly didn't.

Read all about it

As you can imagine, the Bible has quite a lot to say about love. There's a bit in the Bible, in 1 Corinthians 13, that loads of people have read out at their weddings; you might even know it – it starts: 'Love is patient, love is kind. It does not envy, it does not boast, it is not proud.' It's a passage that was used in *Four Weddings and a Funeral* all those years ago, because it's the default choice of most people getting married in church. But it's not specifically about romantic love. When it was written, in about 54CE, the church was new and Christianity in its infancy, so the new, emerging church in the city of Corinth was trying to figure out what it believed and how they were all going to behave. In this passage, St Paul is helping them to understand how they might live in community, together. It's interesting because in English we only have one word for love, but it can mean different types. In Greek there are different words for different types of love: *eros* for erotic love, for example, and *philia* for deep friendship, or *philautia*, which is to do with self-love and self-reliance. But the most common word used in Greek, and used here by St Paul, is *agape*, which is a universal love often used to describe the love of God. It's seen as the highest form of love, which embraces sacrifice and resilience; it's a love that speaks of promise and endurance. Much like being married.

The passage goes on to talk about what love isn't: 'It does not dishonour others, it is not self-seeking, it is not easily angered, it keeps no records of wrongs.' I like to read this as well as the marriage liturgy, which describes marriage and its purpose. It talks about the role of marriage in enriching society and strengthening communities. That really strikes a chord for me, that love is something which builds stronger, better and more stable communities. We think of love as something sentimental and romantic, wishy-washy and touchy-feely, but for me it's also foundational, it's tough and has substance. Love can be concrete and steel as well as silk and velvet.

I say all of this, of course, with my own love and marriage in mind. Graham and I met so long ago neither of us can really remember when it was. I remember seeing him at school one day – I was about fourteen, he was nineteen and had come back to visit his old music teacher. My mate Katie waved at him as he walked across the playground – she knew him from church and because he had taught her the violin. I didn't know anyone who played the violin. My auntie Mary could play the spoons at a wedding if she'd had enough Babycham, but that was about it. He had the most ridiculous haircut, dark curly hair like a microphone, he looked like Leo Sayer. And he was wearing a jumper with a liquorice allsorts pattern on that his mum had knitted him. Heaven only knows what I saw in him. All these years later he might have a better haircut, but he still has a look of Mr Bean.

Anyway, he came over to say hello and I remember thinking he was cute and funny and that church might be somewhere I should go if Graham was going to be there. To be honest, there also wasn't much choice. At youth group we'd been told we shouldn't be 'yoked with unbelievers', meaning dating anyone who wasn't part of the faith was very much frowned upon. Graham had a lovely Christian girlfriend at the time, and as well as being a violin teacher, he was the local vicar's son (just like the Dusty Springfield song), so he wasn't going to be paying much attention to the spotty fourteen-year-old Me. He was away at university when I started taking church more seriously. I dated a couple of boys when I was in sixth form, both called Dave incidentally, neither Christian, so I knew I wouldn't be able to make those relationships serious. But I'd always enjoy catching a glimpse of Graham at church, when he came back for the holidays.

He tells the story of our romance a little differently, of course, reminding me that the thought of romance didn't enter his head until much later – I was after all still in school and he was away at Uni. It was only when we went away after my A levels camping around Europe with one other friend (poor bloke ended up playing gooseberry) that it became more than just a cute friend-ship, and fuelled by tequila and Spanish summer nights we snogged under canvas.

I think we have romanticized ideas about love at first sight. This wasn't that, but I knew there was something I liked about him, probably his weirdness, from the start. I also don't believe in fate or soulmates, or that there's just one person for every person in the world. I believe who we fall in love with is often much more to do with circumstance than the stars aligning. I think that we make the best of the relationship we have with the person we are with. Lifelong partnership is mostly about who is around when you get to the stage in life when you want to make that commitment. In my case, Christian boys were very thin on the ground in my youth. So much so that our little church youth group would go on tour, showing up at other church youth clubs and youth groups whenever we heard that they'd got boys there. A kind of going on the pull for Christian teens. My friends Katie and Nicky both met their future husbands at the Methodist Friday night youth club, across the ping-pong table. I went on Christian holidays and to Christian festivals looking for a Christian boyfriend or at the very least a snog with someone who believed in God. Graham was roughly the right age, a Christian and relatively handsome. We liked lots of the same things. Now, that's not to say that there wasn't a spark – he made me laugh like no one I'd ever met and he liked me, really liked me, just as I was, not taller, or thinner or a watered-down version, but messy and chaotic. I think there needs to be something that piques the interest, a flutter, but often the relationships that stay the distance are the ones that are rooted in some sort of practicality and a shared stoicism, rather than purely in feeling. Romantic? Perhaps not. Practical? Certainly. And I would argue that the act of choosing someone to spend the rest of your days with is so illogical that by its very nature it is incredibly romantic, so why not go into it with your eyes wide open? Feelings are fleeting, and when they're gone what will be left? By all means, fall in love, but give it a fighting chance by making sure it's a practical choice too.

Love can both make perfect sense and at the same time make no sense at all. If you're looking for someone to spend your entire life with until you breathe your last,

I'd challenge anyone who suggests that they know the person is definitely going to stay the course. You can't know, not for certain, but you can be hopeful that they are and you can make sure you have everything working in your favour to make that happen. When I marry two people the truth is that no one there, whether that's the couple, their friends or me, the priest, can know that they will stay the distance, but we are hopeful, we have faith. And that relationship doesn't stay the distance just because the couple want it to; it takes the support of the community. In the marriage service, after the couple have pledged to be faithful to one another for the rest of their lives, they turn to face the family and friends that have gathered to witness their marriage and the priest asks the question, 'Will you, the family and friends of Kyle and Kelley, support and uphold them now and in all the years to come?' To which they answer, 'We will!' I like to practise this with the congregation before the bride gets to church. I've never appeared in a panto-mime (although I can see myself doing a very convincing fairy godmother), so this is the nearest I've got to panto in my professional life. I do the whole 'I'm sure you can do better than that!' and we practise it a few times, but underneath all that frivolity this question has a very ser-ious point. Sometimes the desire of two people to stay together for the rest of their life isn't enough, it's essen-tial that their friends and family commit to do everything to nurture that relationship. It takes more than the will and effort of two people to make a marriage work.

Graham and I recently celebrated our twenty-fifth wedding anniversary. We've lived together in five houses, notched up a handful of degrees, more job changes than I care to count, had two kids, three hamsters and a dog. So, although I'd never consider myself an expert on love, I've mostly been there, done that, and lived to tell the tale. Love is patient. Love is kind, but it's also bloody hard work. The butterfly in love doesn't last for long. Some days you must tell yourself you love them. You have to choose to love them. It starts where your heart skips a beat at the thought of his name and then before you know it you don't like the sound of his breathing and are making him sit in another room to eat his crisps. Lasting love means putting in the work, too.

Love is love

I haven't kept count of how many couples I've married, but it must be a couple of hundred by now. They've all been straight couples though, because of the current (with a capital c) limitations within the Church of England that I touched on earlier.

There are a couple of reasons why same-sex marriage still isn't allowed in the Church of England. First, I guess what you'd call tradition. Marriage has traditionally been between a man and a woman, and those who are opposed to change use the example of marriages in the Bible. They talk about the Holy Family and Adam and Eve, but somehow manage to overlook the fact that not all the examples of marriage in the Bible are that wholesome. Abraham, Moses and David, for example, all had multiple wives and concubines. Marriage back then was more of a civil or legal contract rather than having anything to do with love and fidelity, so to compare one to the other is not really comparing like for like.

The other reason is to do with teachings in the letters from St Paul to the new emerging churches, prohibiting same-sex relationships and encouraging heterosexual monogamy as an indicator and distinguishing feature of the new emerging faith of Christianity. Doing so made it clear that this new religion was not the same as some of the other beliefs and cults that were around at the same time. The trouble with this argument comes when we get into conversations about whether the author of those letters, St Paul, was writing with specific instructions for those churches at that time, or whether these writings are intended to be applied to all Christians for all time.

Some folk argue that you can't cherry-pick which bits of the Bible suit you and which don't, but the truth is we've always done that. The Bible expressly forbids eating prawns and wearing mixed fibres (which is ironic, as I think 99 per cent of clerical cassocks are poly-cotton, the ironing would be unimaginable otherwise!). It also espouses slavery. So, for obvious reasons, we don't take those bits literally. Someone once said to me: 'You don't take the Bible literally so you don't take the Bible seriously,' to which I replied: 'I take the Bible too seriously to take it literally.' The Bible is a book of allegory, poetry, story and illustration, it's not a factual guide book, it's much more beautiful and complicated than that.

Literally or not, the Church of England doesn't move very fast, I'm afraid, and certainly not fast enough for an impatient soul like me. There are denominations that now do same-sex marriage. The Methodists, and the United Reform church, for example. The campaign for equal marriage in the Church of England is doing good work. I was asked to be their patron, but I declined. Not because I don't believe in the cause, not because I don't want to be involved, but because a straight person is not the person to be leading this. I think the best place for a straight person to be is amplifying the voice of the gay community. It's essential that those of us who have privileges use them, of course, but it should never be a distraction drawing focus away from those who are affected directly.

I think change will come as it always does to these things, through conversation, changing culture and dialogue. It is easier to be against something when you don't know someone that represents the thing you're angry about. Take women's ordination, for example. Of course there are still those who don't think women should be ordained, but there are more who do. That changed because people started seeing women doing the job, and saw that it makes sense. It's easy to be angry and against someone whose name you don't know and character you haven't encountered. It might be easy to say, 'I don't think gay people should be allowed to marry,' but it's harder to say that when it's lovely Chris and Steve who live next door and look after your cat when you're away. You get me?

Straight or gay, I can never tell which couples will make it – to the death-do-us-part bit anyway. I've been wrong countless times. There's always a couple who've lived happily together for years and finally tie the knot only for it to end in heartbreak a few weeks later. Or the couples who seem so different you think it'll never work and fifteen years down the line they are still going strong. I once married a couple who had their dog as a ring-bearer – I knew they were going to share a lot of laughter, if nothing else. My point is, what makes marriage last is as mysterious to me as what made them fall in love in the first place. As a vicar it's a big part of my job to facilitate holy matrimony. But at the end of the day, I barely understand my own relationship so I will never presume to understand, or dictate the terms of, anyone else's.

Let's also remember that marriage isn't the be all and end all. I used to think it was. In my early twenties, as part of an evangelical tradition, the expectation was that there was no sex of any sort before marriage. So marriage became something that would absolve me of any guilt from frantic fumbles. The evangelical tradition also taught that marriage and family was the goal and that singleness was second best. I confess my own stupidity at believing this to be true. I confess my own clumsy language around single people at the time.

Marriage was originally a civil exchange more about ownership and money than about love. A practical arrangement, often for financial or feudal security, which developed sacred overtones in order to cement it at the foundation of our society and as the ideal for human happiness. I believe in marriage, really I do, and I think that like any human relationship it can have sacred and holy expressions. But I don't think it has to be the goal for everyone, and I don't think there's one person for one person out there, divinely ordained since before time. Divorce is often sad but sometimes it's not the worst thing to happen.

Love thyself, and others

Love is a choice, and this means more than just the choice to love a romantic partner. The golden rule in pretty much all the major world religions is 'Love your neighbour as you love yourself' or 'Do unto others as you would have them do to you.' It's an emotional quid pro quo, which assumes that a basic level of self-love is present in all of us. Often spiritual leaders focus on the 'loving others' aspect of this tenet, but for me there's also an important caveat here, which is that the way you love others is grounded in the way you love yourself.

How do I mean? Well, it isn't about making sure you

have long hot baths, face packs and a foot spa occasionally, although if that's your thing, more power to you. If you follow me on social media you'll know that my thing is wild swimming, and when I can't get to a river or lake, I jump in a barrel of cold water in my garden for a bit of me-time – it might sound odd but there's something about gritting my teeth and overcoming the cold temperature of the water that provides a welcome distraction and sense of calm which isn't easy to come by. (And yes, I have heard of Wim Hof, the cold-water swimming guru with a cult following. I was asked to appear on his reality TV show *Feel the Freeze* but politely declined. Cold water doesn't scare me, but jumping out of a helicopter is an extreme sport too far.) However you choose to nourish your soul, self-care is not about self-indulgence or inflating your ego with affirmations. Loving yourself is about seeing the inherent value in you as a person.

There's a phrase in my religious tradition, 'God is Love'; the passage goes on to say, 'and those who live in love, live in God and God lives in them'. It's also, incidentally, used in the marriage service. It's a line that tells us that as far as God is concerned, each and every person is valued and loved. It all sounds very nice, doesn't it? It is nice, but for me it's also the single most challenging part of the Christian faith. Why? Because if every person is loved by God and I am to try and love every person, I am therefore compelled to love those who are not always worthy of love. It is the biggest challenge of the Christian faith and, for me, what sets it apart. Even someone who has done something so repulsive that society deems them to be the worst human alive, perhaps even worthy of death, I am challenged to love them. This doesn't mean that they escape judgement or punishment (human or divine), but it does mean that I, because of my faith, am compelled to find some way to love them. To me, this makes the idea of love so much more powerful. The notion that love is a feeling that simply happens to us, over which we have no control, is only one aspect of what love is. So when I talk about 'God is love' I'm not talking about those nice, warm, fluffy feelings of falling in love with someone, or even loving your child or parent. God is Love is, at its core, a fierce and powerful act of defiance, against the notion that someone, anyone, is without worth.

None of which means you can't also feel strong feelings of hate. Love isn't the absence of hate. It's possible to hate someone and their actions but to commit to loving them while your anger exists alongside. Anyone who has raised children knows it is possible to feel more than one thing at once (anyone who hasn't had children can know this too). And when this choice to feel all the feels is made, it brings the power back to the person who has chosen to love, rather than giving all the power to the object of your frustration. Love is the ultimate divine attribute, the essence of what I understand God to be. It's a raging fire of strength that is impossible to quantify and contain. The idea that I am loved by the author of love itself is the foundation of my faith and my reason for everything.

But when Graham eats crisps I still want to squeeze his head.

THREE GOOD THINGS

If love is a choice, it's also a practice. Relationships, even those with ourselves, take work and commitment. Give your loving practice a workout with these three things:

1. **Make a love collage, playlist or Pinterest board.**
   Collect the images, sounds, smells and textures that you associate with loving others and being loved yourself. It might be a colour or a shape, a piece of fabric or a picture from a magazine. Keep it at hand so you can refer to it when you need it. I still have a note my son wrote to me when he was about five years old. In scrawly writing it says, 'Love you Mama'. Whenever I have those panic moments that my bag has gone missing in a restaurant, it's never my phone or wallet I'm scared I've lost but rather that treasured scrap of paper.

2. **Ask different questions.**
   Rather than asking new people you meet if they are married or have kids, ask them instead: 'Who loves you and who do you love?' This is a lovely inclusive conversation starter, leaving it up to the

person to share how much and which information they want, but it also reminds them in that briefest moment that they are loved and they are loving. Love isn't the sole preserve of romance, and we need to talk more about love in all kinds of contexts.

3. **Write an old-fashioned love letter.**
It doesn't need to be to a partner, it can be to anyone you love. Take your time over it, use nice paper if you can (if you can't it doesn't matter) and use your best handwriting, channelling what our grandparents would have done. Nothing can beat a proper letter. You'll make their day, and probably your own too.

3. Strength

More often than not, the way I live my life feels like existing as a human Buckaroo donkey. You know the Buckaroo donkey, right? That children's game where the little plastic donkey is loaded up with miniature lassoes and buckets and cowboy boots and any other random bits of detritus, until the donkey can take the weight no more and kicks off, throwing off all the objects. So it has been with me, and I suspect you too, probably. Each of the things in themselves are small, maybe even fun, but when put on my back with a myriad of other 'small fun tasks', hey, it can tip me over the edge. Yes, I can make the World Book Day costumes, yup absolutely I can do a funeral service next week, sure, I'll cook dinner and so on. I enjoy all of these things in isolation, but one too many and I lose my shit and have to go and sit in the downstairs coat cupboard with a stiff gin. The problem is that we all want to show we're strong and capable all the time; we're afraid to show it when we're feeling worn out and weak – we've confused being strong with being resilient. But I've learned that real strength is so much more complex than that, and I think we can all benefit from seeing the bigger picture, to know that loading yourself up isn't the only way to prove your grit.

We hear a lot about resilience these days, why we all need to be more resilient, and particularly why our kids need to be more resilient. I've even been sent on resilience training for work. There are endless books, courses, YouTube videos and TedTalks that claim to teach us how to be more resilient, and I get it. I know that we need to be ready and able to weather the storms that life inevitably throws at us. But I also think it's an overrated concept. At times it seems to me like the clarion call to be more resilient is really just another way of our society telling us we should be able to take some more shit. Just keep piling it on, seeing how much someone can take, and if anyone complains, tell them they need to be more resilient! This won't be news to many of you readers, but I notice women being lumbered with more than men. We seem to like calling women strong, as though that accolade will make things easier to bear, or that recognition is what they are hoping for.

I prefer to talk about strength in a much broader capacity (not the physical kind, although that's pretty good, and often the two are linked, but right now I mean the emotional kind). Resilience is an isolated quality, it's all on you, whereas strength is communal, it compounds. Strength is infectious. If you think about it, it's a kind of conductor for all the other good emotions and qualities: kindness, empathy, patience – they all get turbo-charged by strength.

In the Christian tradition that I belong to, strength is continually shown by those who are perceived as weak.

79

One of the Bible's most well-known stories, about David the shepherd boy who kills the giant Goliath, is the perfect example. Similarly, in the resurrection story, in the moments of Jesus's death, it wasn't the strong former fishermen disciples who were pressed into action, it was the apparently 'weak' women. It was Mary Magdalene, the apostle to the apostles, the one who was sent with the message to those who would then take the message even further. Mary M is the original, and was also the first witness to the resurrection. Time and again, the Bible teaches the lesson that we should not dismiss those who we perceive to be weak as being without strength and power. In fact, the Bible is full of women of strength, it's just that you probably haven't heard about them.

In the Old Testament there's the brilliant but gruesome story of Jael, a woman who offers hospitality to an army general, Sisera, then drives a tent peg into his head while he sleeps. Incidentally, technically Jael is on the same side as Sisera, but she doesn't like the way he's gone about things and the oppression that has been inflicted on the opposition, so despite being perceived as non-threatening she comes into her own. A song written partly in praise of Jael's actions is widely thought to be one of the oldest parts of the Bible. And then there's Judith, mentioned in the Apocrypha, who grows weary of her countrymen's weakness in war, and takes matters into her own hands, by wooing the enemy general, getting him drunk and decapitating him while he sleeps. She takes the head back to her own armies, plonks it down and says, 'That's how you do it,' and vows never to marry. Or the low-status concubine Rizpah, whose sons were killed by David (yes, that sweet giant-killing boy David, now all grown-up and a tyrannous king with more issues than *Vogue*) and their corpses displayed by being hung on the city walls. Rizpah kept vigil over their decomposing bodies, beating away the wild animals and shouting at the carrion birds for five months, until David gave permission to allow them to be properly buried. These unfamiliar stories are bumped for what might be considered the 'more palatable' tales like Noah's Ark and the heroic David and Goliath, although in truth those stories too have gory bits that are skipped over (for example, Noah got drunk and naked as the zebras disembarked). Perhaps the accounts of the women have been skipped over because they are more brief than the other male 'lead' stories. Or perhaps it's because boys are typically considered better role models and we'd rather the Sunday school kids heard about them? Truth is, I'd much rather be a Rizpah than a Noah.

In the gospels, Jesus uses another symbol of weakness as strength, saying that to get into the kingdom of heaven you must become like a little child. He says in Matthew: 'I tell you the truth, unless you change and become like little children, you will never enter the kingdom of heaven. Therefore, whoever humbles himself like this child is the greatest in the kingdom of heaven. And whoever welcomes a little child like this in my name welcomes me.' Jesus was always turning things around to make the least expected statements, like 'Blessed are they who mourn,' and 'The meek will inherit the earth.' He was a big fan of the idea that children and those who hold little power will eventually be the most powerful. As a man he was also the opposite of what was expected: a Messiah is supposed to be a great political and military leader, and instead he's a builder's son from a rural backwater. Time and again it is those with little or no power who Jesus seeks to elevate. Over the years I've heard sermons suggesting that in his encouragement for us to become like children, Jesus wants us all to remain innocent and vulnerable and to hold on to that same childlike naivety, to blindly believe without asking too many questions. I don't know which children those preachers know, but when my kids were little they were constantly questioning everything. 'Why?' is a two-year-old's favourite word. So perhaps when Jesus suggests embracing the faith of children to gain access to heaven, it's less about blind acceptance and more about adopting an enquiring mind, maybe even embracing a toddler's exuberance, and propensity to disrupt.

Being faith-curious

Now I think about it, perhaps the route to strength is about being even more playful with our faith. Lots of people tell me they are not religious but still find religion interesting. I think this is a really valid and important point of view, one that society needs to make more space for. Just as people can describe themselves as sober-curious or divorce-curious, we should allow people the permission to be faith-curious and discover how that might help them, without dismissing them as 'non-religious'.

After all, reading the Bible rarely converts anyone to Christianity, and often it raises more questions than answers. And because of translation and cultural context it's not exactly an easy or thrilling read. Often, people try to read the Bible like a novel, starting at the beginning and trying to read to the end. But the Bible isn't supposed to be read like *Gone Girl* – sorry to disappoint if you'd been planning it for your next beach read. First of all, it's sixty-six books, not one, so those who try to read it like a story usually find it impenetrable. What I say to people who try to read the Bible is: you don't need to believe all of it or even to understand all of it in order to find the stories and teachings helpful. And don't be embarrassed about wanting to read a Bible, even if it's just out of curiosity and even if it doesn't always make sense. And, as I say, if you're looking for a page-turner, anything by Gillian Flynn is probably a safer bet.

The Bible teaches us that strength lies in being meek and childlike, or maybe even not feeling certain about our faith. In many schools and pre-schools we sing hymns about this and teach children the stories of humility and kindness. And yet we seem so often to struggle with walking that talk. We hide our emotions, put on a brave face, especially when others are being unkind to us.

I was called names a lot at school. Being short, round, ginger and Christian meant I was a walking field day for bullies. The tactic I was always told to employ by friends, family and church was not to show them I was rattled. I was to walk tall, with my head held high, and to repeat to myself the old 'sticks and stones' adage. It didn't work, of course. Whoever came up with that rhyme quite clearly had never been properly beaten up for refusing to let someone else copy their homework, or picked on for having shit generic shoe-shop trainers. I hated being picked on and I hated that I couldn't stop it.

Bullying followed me into adulthood. It might surprise you to hear that churches can be very bullying spaces. There are a lot of folk vying for status in organized religion, even, or especially, in the small towns and rural villages of sleepy England. Often the church council is made up of retired people, who have become accustomed to being deferred to at work, and often at home. So, when someone younger than their daughter comes along and tries to lead them, they don't like it. Heels are dug in, tutting sounds are made and before long getting any sort of decision made or change facilitated becomes impossible. I used to think giving as good as I got was the answer, to become immovable myself, two stags locking horns and seeing who could push the other over. I've learned that this tactic rarely works and, if it does, rarely delivers a happy peace. Rather, one person has to lose face and limp away injured while the other reluctantly raises the trophy to faint applause. Fighting isn't always the strong person's move. Sometimes we have to have the foresight to spot the wave coming towards us, widen our stance, brace ourselves, know that it will knock us off our feet for a while, and have faith that it will pass and we will surface from it. Perhaps a little shaken, a bit breathless and disoriented, but still breathing, in and out, ready to face the next wave.

A big part of my job is curating a space for others to be vulnerable, to allow themselves to open up and feel fully supported by me. I've become a bit of a pro at this, but I still have to remind myself that it's OK to be vulnerable too, as it can lead to the most valuable type of strength. This always comes to the fore when I have to do a funeral that is especially difficult. Of course I need to be professional and competent, but in displaying my own emotions and how the situation is affecting me it can help give texture and tone to what is happening. People often talk about feeling numb when someone dies, and so sometimes my job as the person helping to navigate for the family is to help them make sense of that numbness. In particularly tragic deaths, that numbness is even more pronounced, the subconscious perhaps anaesthetizing the emotional response to aid survival. I've done funerals for people who have taken their own lives and for victims of murder, including children and babies. Rather shockingly, my first funeral for someone who had been murdered was for a child just a few months old, whose father was suspected of killing her. Vulnerability here was vital, coupled with professionalism and practicality. Something the local funeral director knew instinctively.

'I need someone soft,' said the funeral director when he called to give me the job. It was his slightly awkward way of saying he needed someone who could allow themselves to be alongside this family and engage with the enormity of the situation as they came to terms with the reality of what had happened. Of course, it makes sense to me now; he needed someone who would empathize, not just come in and do 'the God bit'.

When there's been a death, the funeral director will get in touch to ask for my availability. Anyone can have their funeral in church – of course it has to be a Christian service, but you don't have to be a regular attendee or a communicant member. Funeral directors usually get in touch by phone call, but most of my local funeral directors have learned that I'm not great at answering my phone (more on this later) and have cottoned on that if they text me I'll text them back almost immediately. Once the funeral director and I have arranged a date, time and place for the service, I'll phone the family and arrange a time to go and see them. This is usually in their home. They'll be nervous, usually, and often curtain-twitching. But that visit is where we get to talk about the person who has died and I can hear their story. Driving to see the parents for that initial visit, I asked myself what on earth I could bring to this situation. The circumstances and facts of what had happened were not yet clear; all I knew was that a baby was dead, her father was out on bail and her mother didn't think he'd done it. I knew they wanted the funeral done before the trial. The mother had been out of the house when it happened, she'd popped out for nappies and a bit of a break, and when she came home the ambulance was on its way. We didn't know what was going to happen next in terms of a trial, but that wasn't my job here. I'd helped families grieving the loss of their children before, but this was a nuanced and complex set of circumstances that by its nature involved the law, and with that, a potential prison sentence for the baby's dad. Everyone was scared, me included, word had got out into the community and there were many who wanted to exert their own kind of justice on the baby's father, so the family had been moved to a safe house for their own protection, and everyone was going to need to find a strength they didn't know they had.

With no available instruction booklet for this kind of event, I decided that all I could do was simply be there for this family who had lost their baby, a mum and a dad who were going through the unimaginable. My judgements, and those of society, would stay on the front doorstep while I was with them. I knew I had no words, religious or otherwise, that could comfort them, but that my simple willingness to sit alongside them without judgement was the only comfort of sorts that I could offer. When words and deeds fail, there is a power in just being with someone. I use this all the time when visiting the dying, resist the urge to try to find words to say and actions to do, but just be present.

It was in accepting my own vulnerability that I was able to navigate the tensions and emotions of such a sad funeral and use my experience to be strong for the family. In acknowledging that I had no words of condolence to offer these people, that this was a problem with no solution, I was able to step into my role and be the person this family needed to lean on over those acutely difficult few days. The mum fought the accusation of her husband as the killer as hard as she could. When we talked in that first meeting, most of what she wanted to say was about his innocence; my job was to pull the conversation around to be about the baby. I wasn't here as a police officer, or a judge, but as someone helping them say goodbye to their baby. When you do a baby funeral it's different from an adult service in so many ways, but one is that a eulogy, where you list the dead person's achievements (remember this never includes your dress size or the state of your skirting boards), doesn't seem quite right. So instead you talk about the pregnancy, the birth, favourite toys and music and TV shows. We looked at scan pictures and first photos. I hugged them both, something I don't think anyone else outside family and friends had been able to do – police and funeral directors tend to be more impartial; the hug was tight and long and we cried. I felt useful, I felt like I was in the right place at the right time for the right reason. I remembered Jesus sitting with people excluded by society, spending time with criminals and thieves, and during that time I felt more like a representative of Christ than I ever had, or have since.

Later on, when the baby's father did go to prison, I felt sorry for him. That sounds weird, right? Or even wrong. He killed a baby, after all. But clearly something had gone really wrong here, not just in the moment of the act but perhaps too in his background. I didn't like the idea of him alone, with no one to sit with him. That doesn't mean I don't think he shouldn't have gone to prison, or that he shouldn't be expected to somehow make amends for what he'd done, as if that would be possible. But having spent time with him I knew that the pain he was suffering because of what had happened was like nothing else I've ever witnessed. He was a bad person who had done a bad thing, but I have to believe was worthy of an opportunity for redemption and worthy of love, that's the challenge of my faith. I wrote to him in prison and requested a visit, which he declined. I found that really difficult – I think perhaps because I wanted to know the end of the story, but also because I didn't know if he had anyone to talk to and be alongside him. Did he have a friend? Why was it so tough for me that a convicted murderer didn't want to meet me? When I think about him now and the situation we all found ourselves in that day, I feel immensely sad, obviously first for the child, but also for him, though not in the same way of course. It was an absolute tragedy, with nothing to redeem it. The situation was so desperate, so dire, so utterly devastating and helpless, devoid of any glimmer of restoration. I suppose that was why I wanted so much to visit him. I wanted to check he was as OK as he could be and make him feel less alone in his pain. Strength, when a fellow human being is at their absolute weakest, is not about demonstrating power or invincibility, it's about sharing their vulnerability. Strength and vulnerability are two sides of the same coin. I'll never know why he chose not to see me, but I hope he knew he wasn't alone.

Just being there, sitting with someone in their moment of need without trying to 'fix', is a really powerful thing. I go into quite a few care homes with my work – something I used to be quite scared of, before I got to know more people with disabilities and atypical cognitive function. I felt embarrassed and didn't know what I was supposed to say to people, I found myself trying to fill the silences with small talk and chit-chat, embarrassed and awkward in the silence. I've learned over the years, and by being told to shut up a few times, that I don't need to put on a show, and that sometimes just sitting with a person is all I need to do to make them feel someone is with them.

The Jewish faith really has this technique down to a fine art. In Judaism, when someone dies, close friends and family come to 'sit shiva' with them for a week. People literally come round and sit on low chairs in a room with the mourning person or family in their house, their physical presence and time together being the conduit of strength, not words or fancy ceremonies, just good, solid being there. I'm not Jewish, so I've never sat shiva. The nearest I've come to it is dropping round to a friend's with a lasagne when someone they love dies. But the sentiment, in a small way, is kind of the same, it's about solidarity. I also like that in Judaism, there is a set pattern of what mourning looks like; there are rules to follow, a structure. I think this helps with the sense of impotence we all feel around death, that feeling that we don't know what to do or say. It's a feeling so uncomfortable that people will cross the road – literally and metaphorically – in order to avoid seeing or being with someone who is grieving. I don't know if this is unique to British culture. Shiva means everyone knows what they are supposed to do, it supports the supporters. I'm getting a bit ahead of myself here, as the whole final chapter is on grief, but it is kind of my specialist subject and I think this is an important lesson on how we can draw strength in life's hardest moments, so I hope you'll let me off.

A marathon, not a sprint

Of course, strength isn't only something we need to roll out at funerals or for people on their deathbeds in hospitals and nursing homes. For some of us, finding and providing our inner strength for others, and for ourselves, is something we do every single day – it's a marathon not a sprint.

My son, Arthur, is neurodiverse. People don't always know what that means, but we decided against a medical diagnosis of autism, which would involve a hospital visit. Arthur isn't ill, he doesn't have a condition that needs to be cured. I understand it's more complicated than that, and it's different for everyone, but that's what felt right for us. The term 'neurodiverse' speaks less of some kind of deficit in Arthur, and celebrates his differences. He did have an educational diagnosis at school and received extra help and time in class, but the idea of taking him to a doctor or a hospital about something that is such an essential part of who he is seemed ridiculous. He's eighteen now and is thinking about the idea of a diagnosis for himself, and if that's something he goes ahead with, we'll support him in it.

Being blessed with neurodiversity means Arthur looks at the world a little differently. But as he says himself: 'What if I'm the normal one?' He doesn't make friendships easily but when he does he is the loyallest friend you could hope for. He doesn't like doing things he isn't interested in, but when he does find something he is interested in he finds out everything he can about it and will happily and keenly share that knowledge with anyone who will listen. He never forgets information that he enjoys, but forgets almost everything he has no interest in. He finds passing exams tricky and writing essays difficult, he can't ride a bike or tie his shoelaces, but he can remember facts about rollercoasters like no one I've ever met.

Being a mum to a child who you worry the world won't understand is hard. Seeing people be outwardly hostile to him, and ridicule him, is not something anyone wants to go through. It can feel like every day you send him out into the world, you're sending him out to the lions. It's painful. Parenting any child requires strength, and parenting a child in a world that won't allow that child to fit requires the strength of a concrete elephant. And I realize that after all I said about vulnerability and strength being perfected in weakness, this sounds like a contradiction, but there's a stoicism needed as well as a gentleness in parenting kids with additional needs. And I don't mean you need to be stoic to deal with your child, but rather to not be ground down by the limits society puts on them.

It also goes without saying, though, that there are some wonderful moments that come with being his mum. Graham and I tried recently to teach Arthur about the concept of double-entendres and how they work in everyday conversations. The nuances and implied meanings of our everyday conversations can be really hard for neurodiverse people to recognize and interpret. In our house when a double-entendre crops up (which they do surprisingly often) we say: 'Sounds like my wedding night!' It's quite a tricky concept when you think about it, and Arthur just couldn't quite work it out. I would ask: 'Would you like pizza for tea?' and he'd reply: 'Sounds like my wedding night.' Not quite, son. But a few days later, we were in the supermarket and I took my bank card out of the machine before the transaction had gone through. 'You pulled it out too soon,' said the cashier. 'Sounds like my wedding night?' said Arthur. Boom! High fives and back slaps all round. Lord knows what the cashier thought.

You have to get good at celebrating the little things like that, the things that might seem unimportant to other people. And you have to learn to tag team. The sheer longevity of the kind of strength required in our family, and in the family of anyone whose load feels heavier, and differently distributed, than others', means taking regular breaks. I have Graham to tag team with, so we can share out the little everyday struggles that we have with Arthur, whether that's simple stuff like getting dressed or harder stuff like navigating friendships. I feel very blessed to have Graham and the relationship we share, our daughter Ruby too, and if I didn't, I know I'd need to find someone else to tag team with. I couldn't do it all alone. It is in acknowledgement of my vulnerability that I'm able to find and accept the help and strength that I need to keep going.

But also Arthur is a blessing to our family. Completely and utterly wonderful. Often the way he sees the world is much more compassionate and interesting than a neurotypical person. He doesn't binge box sets, but

spreads them out over weeks enjoying the delayed grat-
ification; as a little boy he'd take months to open his
Christmas presents, finishing playing with one toy before
opening another. When my mum was dying, we asked if
he'd like to go to the hospital to say goodbye, thinking
he might be frightened, but he didn't flinch and said
without hesitation, 'Grandad is going to need me.' In
these priceless moments every worry for my brilliant
son seems to matter a little less.

The reality is that life is a series of challenges and you
never know when the next one is going to come along
and test you; like a never-ending assault course, it seems
like we've just dragged ourselves through one mud-
soaked cargo net only to find a ten-foot brick wall and a
rope that demands our attention on the other side. You
have to keep a kind of stealth strength in reserve that
you know you can whip out when required. And, just
like a weightlifter or bodybuilder, this kind of strength
needs training for. It needs building and maintaining.

How you do that is an entirely personal thing. For me,
it often means cocooning myself. I've already mentioned
my propensity for sitting inside a big barrel of freezing
cold water and the sense of calm that process gives me.
But I also have a cupboard under the stairs, the one with
the coats in, where I go to literally curl up and recharge.
I switch off all my settings, the ones on my phone and
the ones in my head, pull all the coats around me, tune
out the noise and kerfuffle of family life going on outside, and sit there quietly until I feel able to go outside

again. It's a kind of mini-hibernation that usually only lasts about the length of two KitKat Chunkies but gets me through until the next time I feel low on power.

Other people I know run, cycle, knit, flower-arrange, collect Dr Who figures, play board games, paraglide and surf – not all at the same time, that would be ridiculous. But it's all the same thing really, isn't it? A sort of meditation, an attempt to reboot the connection with yourself and find purpose and peace.

Stepping back from the bigger picture

'The world is a scary place right now.' You hear a lot of people say that. It's undeniably true that we are experiencing some serious turbulence as a human race, and as inhabitants of planet Earth. As I write this the effects of climate change are becoming a stark reality, with the UK recently having experienced its hottest EVER day. It feels like just staying positive takes a lot of strength these days.

It's hard to stay hopeful in times like these, to be strong enough on our own to keep the faith, and believe that there is still time to turn the ship around. Sometimes you have to take a step back from it all. Because when you think about it, the world is pretty much always experiencing some sort of terror, and triumph, at any given moment. And while you can't do anything immediately to solve this huge existential threat, you can adjust the way you respond to it.

When I find myself getting caught up in the news cycle or feeling overwhelmed by things going on outside of my control, I remind myself of the advice I learned years ago from one of my very best friends. They have a problematic relationship with alcohol. Let's not dress it up – in their own words, they are an alcoholic and always will be. I won't name them, although they probably wouldn't mind if I did. They are generous and kind enough to know that by owning their addiction they can help others. On paper my friend has everything going for them. They have status and wealth, they are fairly posh (I know that will mean different things to different people, but there's a Sir and Lady in the family), so you might assume that they lived a charmed life free of worries. But at the heart of their community of family and friends lies a toxic drinking culture which, if not the cause of their alcoholism, was becoming a serious problem for them. They struggled to navigate this for years but eventually decided to stand up for themselves and their health and turn their back on the drinking culture in which they were raised. With a huge house to retreat to, no one would mind very much or even notice if my friend carried on drinking, so long as the house and the business stood standing. Others in the same position have chosen that path, but my friend chose the more difficult path of sobriety. When I think about strength, they are the first person that comes to mind. My friend is strong because the demon who seeks to make them weak and rob them of hope has been named and owned.

In the end my friend had done what was right for them, and after realizing that they couldn't control the reactions of their friends or family they developed a mantra to repeat in those moments and keep them grounded: 'Where are your feet?'

I have found this phrase so valuable in those moments when life feels in flux, when the bigger picture feels too overwhelming to contemplate. Asking yourself, 'Where are your feet?' gets you to focus on something smaller and more immediate. It asks: 'What's happening right now?' 'Am I safe?' 'Am I loved?' 'Am I going to eat today?' Life is of course more than just these things, but an audit of the circumstances you find yourself in can help you take a minute to assess what is important and keep things in perspective. It's the good old-fashioned 'Will this matter in five years' time?' or taking a second to count blessings. This isn't to downplay the climate change, or war, pandemic, recession, or politics we see just now. But rather to suggest that the world has never been a place of peace and harmony, and yet we remain hopeful. The world has always been utterly chaotic, and yet here we are still having children and planning our futures.

Hopefully you can use 'Where are your feet?' as a meditation, a rallying cry and a centring exercise, all rolled into one, like me and my friend do. It's a brilliant way of distracting yourself away from your worries and fears, right back to the present moment. When I rock up to their house in a rage about something that's happened at home, or work, or both, after raging gently with me for a moment, they'll ask: 'Where are your feet?' And I instantly feel better, more focused, stronger.

Avengers assemble

Ultimately, we can all be our own versions of strong, and we can find our strength in cupboards or mantras, but without being connected to others we will always be only a tiny, isolated link, more exposed to life's curveballs.

I like to think I'm a good friend – don't we all? Like most of us, I've got old, old friendships that have been going longer than I care to count, and I've had other, deeper friendships that have lasted only a short time. Some friendships seem to mature with you while others fade as you change and grow. It's always sad when that happens, so I have to remind myself that it's really normal. No one is the same person they were ten years ago when I met them, and neither am I. Some of my friendships were built around a specific period in my life – especially the early years of motherhood – and were born out of necessity and survival. Vicar school was only two years, so my friendships there were made quickly. Years later, what at the time seemed like an unbreakable bond is now played out almost exclusively on social media. This doesn't make it any less true, of course.

It'll probably surprise you when I say I used to find

myself lost for words, especially in tragic situations. I remember a friend I had been to school with being diagnosed with cancer in her early twenties. To my shame I put off contacting her for weeks. I didn't know how to talk about her illness and I absolutely didn't want to say the wrong thing. Luckily this is something that I've learned to navigate now (I wouldn't be a very good vicar if I hadn't!), but I know I'm not the only one who has felt like this. Those who have been bereaved often describe to me how they see folk crossing the road to avoid them, or feel like invitations to nights out are drying up because their friends feel awkward around them. I think the problem is that we put too much pressure on ourselves. Chances are the person with life-changing news doesn't know how to feel or act or think either, so we need to stop shying away from the elephant in the room and show our support in any way we can.

I learned the secret to this the hard way. When we were in our twenties, my friend Katie was pregnant and her baby died. Everyone in our friendship group was having babies and I simply didn't know what to say. So I did the only thing that I knew could lighten her load even for an hour: I made a lasagne. I took it round, handed it over, hugged her and left. I felt like a coward for not staying. Years later Katie told me that lasagne was one of the best things anyone did for her on that crappest of crap days. Since then it has become my failsafe for when any BIG stuff happens. Death? Lasagne. Birth? Lasagne. House move? New job? End of the world? Lasagne. I know this might seem obvious and I'm very much aware that I haven't just cracked a formula that will win me a Nobel Peace Prize (though I do think lasagne is worthy of one), but I think this story is a helpful reminder that showing you are there for someone can take many forms.

We put pressure on ourselves to be the best possible friend to all our friends all the time, especially when we're younger, but this can end up causing frustration when it isn't reciprocated and stress when we don't feel like we can live up to expectations. How can we be strong for others when we don't even have time for ourselves? I've learned that the key is not to overthink it and not to say, 'If you need anything just call,' because invariably the person can't articulate what they need. Instead, do something. Simply reaching out from the void, whether that's with a text, a wave at the school gates or a delivery of lasagne, is better than nothing, so don't put pressure on yourself to be the queen of grand gestures. And when in doubt – feed.

When lasagne doesn't cut it

When I pray (yes, we do do that, and no, I don't have to be on my knees with my hands clasped together on my bed wearing a frilly nightie, although I did try that once when I was feeling particularly pious one Lent; it didn't last long, the kids found it hilarious), strength is the quality I pray for most often. One of my favourite hymns has the line, 'Strength for today and bright hope for tomorrow.' And it's also true that many a non-believer has called on their invisible God when they've needed courage. Maybe you count yourself in this number and I'm pleased to tell you that it's OK; no one – even God – thinks you're a cheat. It's no surprise that when we experience true desperation and fear with no physical solution we turn to the metaphysical. And I'm no exception. Being religious doesn't make anyone immune to bad stuff happening; I've asked for strength many times in my life. This was especially true when my mum had a massive heart attack and when my dad was diagnosed with cancer. I only wish religion was like a comic book hero shield protecting me from feeling frightened. Truth is, life is often just as terrifying for those who believe as for those who don't.

Back in 2006 my mum had a heart attack – she was taken into intensive care, it was serious and there were questions around her survival. Within hours of her being admitted, myself and my vicar at the time went along and anointed her and prayed with her as the ventilator tube inflated her lungs, and I stroked her hair and told her not to be frightened. Anointing with holy oil and prayer is common practice, hoping for recovery but covering the spiritual bases in case the worse should happen; it's sometimes linked with what you might have heard called 'the last rites'. I was once called to a parishioner's hospital bedside as a young curate and realized once on the ward that I'd forgotten the holy oil. Riffling through my handbag, I had to use the only thing I had that might make a passing substitute: muttering the prayers, I made the sign of the cross on the gentleman's forehead with hand cream. No one ever knew and he lived for another sixteen weeks.

The day after my mum was taken to hospital I was due to go to my residential interview to see if they'd let me go on to train to be a vicar; it's called a BAP: Bishop's Advisory Panel. It was to be three days of interviews, which of course I would now miss because I wanted to be by my mum's side. But my dad wasn't going to let that happen. He didn't want me to miss what felt like my one chance of following my calling and embracing the vocation that my heart was set on, so I was sent away to my BAP, knowing that there was a chance my mum wouldn't be in the world when I got back. A tiny selfish part of me was glad to not be there – that sounds terrible, doesn't it? But I just wanted to go to my cupboard and hide from everything that was scary, and somehow being psychometrically tested to see if I'd make a good vicar seemed easier than standing at my mum's bedside as she died.

She hung on, no better, no worse, and once I was back from my BAP, me and my aunties frequently visited the hospital chapel, pausing to write my mum's name in the book at the back of the chapel for prayer requests. We spent hours and days as a family sitting in those bloody awful relative rooms (they aren't awful, of course, but no amount of watercolours and fresh flowers changes what those rooms are for). My dad and my big strong uncles, Edward, David, John, Trevor and George, stood with bloodshot eyes waiting for the door to open and the worst of news to come in. The days spread into weeks. Despite being the so-called 'religious one' in my family, I found praying really hard in those dark days. If I prayed for my mum to get better and she didn't, then what sort of witness would I be for my faith? Where would my faith even be if my mum died? So I developed a standard Anglican fudge of a prayer.

'Lord, if it is your will, heal Margaret, whether in this life or the next.'

My auntie Mary took great exception to this prayer and countered it with her own, more forthright 'Jesus, when tha were on earth, tha did miracles. We need one. Do one.'

If my prayer was made of fudge, hers was forged in steel. Words of defiant confidence, expressed with economy, that everyone needed to hear. While I couldn't find the right words, her prayer came from a place of strength in a moment of shared vulnerability, fear and weakness. Sadly it is so often only in these challenging moments that the strength we didn't know we had becomes apparent. A strong woman's simple request gave us all a new determination to go back on to the ward and face what was next, even if that was my mum's death.

One morning just after breakfast the call came, THAT call. 'Come now.' Graham was at work, I had a two-year-old and a four-year-old both covered in Weeta-bix, still in their pyjamas. I tipped them into the car and drove to my friend Denise's. Den is Ruby's godmother. She's gobby, loud, forthright and righteous. (We decided early on that it was better to make Den a godmother and have her on our team than to risk not having her in our corner, because I'd hate to have to face her down in a fight. Her strength of character and unwavering sense of right and wrong meant she'd argue with God on the cross if she felt she had to.) Her son Joel was just a few weeks older than Ruby but she had still agreed to look after Ruby for us when I'd first gone back to work as a teacher – needless to say, Den was a legend. So on this fateful morning I pulled up outside Den's house, I didn't turn off the engine, I just lifted the kids out of the car and put them in her front garden. Alerted by the sound of the car, Den came out of her front door, and before she even had a chance to say hello I was back in the car and driving to the hospital. Luckily mum was a trooper and she pulled through that day, and when I got back to Den's much, much later, the children I'd dropped off, Weetabix-encrusted and semi-naked, were dressed, fed and had had a wonderful day playing with their god-brother Joel. I remember Denise catching my eye, and without saying anything she gave me a look that said she was in my corner, that I could get on with the business of finding strength to face whatever I was facing. Friend-ship sometimes means asking no questions. Strength comes in the silences.

Mum was with us for another sixteen glorious years and we finally said our goodbyes to her in January of 2023. I'd like to say enormous thanks to the NHS staff who continued to care for her until her last breath. Although she was forever changed by her experience and life wasn't quite the same after that, perhaps Auntie Mary's prayers made all the difference. If they did, then it raises the question of why God seems to answer some prayers and not others. Or is it that we only notice when the answer is the one we want to hear? The saying goes that God always answers our prayers, it's just that sometimes the answer is 'no'. It's a great mystery of faith if ever there was one. What I do know is that Mum's illness led to a kind of renaissance of faith in our family, with most of the women who gathered at that bedside subsequently deciding to get confirmed at church. (Confirmation is a ceremony in the church when adults take on the promises made when they were christened as babies for themselves. For many, me included, it's the first time you formally stand up and say, 'This is what I believe.')

There have been times, especially in the early days of her recovery, when it looked like Mum might never manage solid food ever again. She was being fed through a tube and we wondered whether it might have been kinder for our prayers to be answered in a different way. But as my uncle David used to say, 'We are where we are.' If God answers prayers, I believe God is there when someone we love is ill and dying. But I've come to realize that we can't think of praying like ordering pizza, where we get to specify our order and complain if it doesn't arrive on time with the topping of our choice. What it comes down to for me is that because Jesus was human (as well as, for Christians, divine), it means that at the core of my faith is a belief that somehow the ultimate source of love in the universe understands and has felt human suffering and death, and while that might not make it easier it does mean that somehow there's a solidarity and God is in it with us. I take huge comfort in that. It doesn't mean I don't get mad at God, though. Jesus got mad at him, too. When he was on the cross he shouted, 'My God, my God, why have you forsaken me?' And if Jesus can feel abandoned by God, alone, wondering where the hell God has gone, then I think we all can.

Most of the uncles and aunts that gathered at her bedside, along with her, have died; we've gathered at their bedsides, I've done their funerals. The funeral of a family member is always a 'Where are your feet?' sort of day. There's usually a lasagne involved. Champagne helps, too. When my friend Jean was dying, she asked me how I would do my grieving once the funeral – which I had the honour of conducting – was over. I said I wanted to go home and watch *Downton Abbey*, and drink a bottle of champagne all to myself. When I arrived home after the service, emotionally exhausted and sad to have lost my friend, I saw a basket on the front doorstep with a bottle of champagne inside and a note on the neck that simply said, 'You'll need this.' One classy lady, was Jean.

As Scarlett O'Hara once said: 'Tomorrow is another

day.' When strength seems to elude you, this simple fact can buoy you until it returns. It's a sense of moving forward, towards hope. The reading we had at our wedding was: 'Do not worry about tomorrow, for tomorrow has enough worries of its own.' It was in the King James version of the Bible, which was translated from the original Greek as: 'Sufficient unto the day is the evil thereof.' Today's troubles are enough, so always remember, where are your feet?

THREE GOOD THINGS

Strength needs building and maintaining. Here are three things you can do to help boost yours, and the strength of those around you:

1. **Find your feet.**
   Take off your shoes and socks (if you're wearing tights I'll let you off) – get someone to help you if you need to. Ask yourself, 'Where are your feet?' (or hands, or elbows, or whatever other body part might help you) and begin to list in your head the things you can see happening right now. For example: 'There's a man in a white shirt.' 'There's a table.' 'There's a chair.' This sounds incredibly basic and simplistic and in many ways it is, but it's a practice that has helped me, usually when I'm getting into cold water, to name what I'm seeing and feeling and to take away the fear of the unknown and unnamed.

Listening to and touching what I can see and what I feel calms me and focuses me.

2. **Think of the strongest person you know.**
What is it that makes them strong? When have you been at your strongest, emotionally, physically, spiritually? What did it look like? Now imagine putting that strength into storage or on ice, for a time when you will need it. Knowing you've got it there to access whenever you need to can be reassuring. It can help to draw this image as well – get a sketchbook and draw a picture of how the freezer might look with all these attributes packed in and accessible at any time.

3. **Push yourself.**
Stretch your strength by deliberately trying something that scares you; take a friend with you for support. Set challenges for yourself that take you outside of your comfort zone. Ever fancied having a go at boxing? Get down to your local club. Want to travel alone but worried about how you'll get by? Book the ticket and go for it. My friend Sarah had a year of saying 'Go on then' whenever she was invited to something. Documenting these challenges on social media or in a family WhatsApp group is a great way to keep yourself accountable and make sure you don't back out. But understand that the strength you're looking for might be found in failing those challenges rather than in succeeding.

4. Conflict

When I was a little girl, I accidentally knocked the head off one of my mum's favourite ornaments, a statuette of a little girl feeding a flock of geese. I found some Blu Tack and quickly stuck her head back on. It was a bit wonky but no one noticed at first and I managed to get away with it for a few weeks. However, I knew the day was coming when Mum would go round with the duster and my crime would be discovered. But rather than admit my mistake, I tried to avoid the inevitable telling-off. I still remember that feeling of anxious anticipation in my tummy, like I'd had a washing machine fitted inside me. I was terrified of conflict, and still am. We all know someone who seems to want to pick a fight at every possible opportunity, but, for most of us, conflict is something we do everything we can to avoid. It's uncomfortable and makes us feel we're not safe.

I'd like to say that gut-wrenching feeling is something I've never had since I knocked that ornament over, but the truth is that I've had fallouts and made mistakes over the years, and every now and again I revisit them and the feeling comes back. Perhaps you know the feeling too? I remember when I resigned from one of my parishes. The convention is that you go and tell your churchwardens that you are leaving before you announce it to the congregation on Sunday morning. So ahead of my big announcement, I went to my wardens' houses to tell them the news that I was moving on. It was all confidential, the churchwardens – who, incidentally, were both called Martin – were sworn to secrecy. I told them my plans and thought nothing more about it. Until later that evening when I got home and waiting for me was an answerphone message from the landlord of the pub saying how sorry he was that I was leaving. It turned out he'd heard someone talking about it in the Co-op, and they'd heard it from the previous vicar, who'd been told by the churchwarden. Incensed, I dialled the warden's number but he wasn't in. I left a ranting message on his answerphone about how angry I was that he'd been gossiping my news around the village ahead of the official announcement. Slamming the phone down, I felt like justice had been delivered, but, you guessed it, I had the wrong Martin. I still live in the same area and that means I occasionally bump into the 'wrong' one who I'd given an earful to at the supermarket. Except I don't, because I usually hide until he's gone. So hideous is the memory of my huge and very angry mistake, I can't face seeing him. I handled that conflict very badly.

Over the years I've become better at managing my response to conflict. I yell less than I used to, certainly at innocent churchwardens anyway, and I am more willing to let things go. I recently got shouted at in a car park by a woman who was certain I had messed up her electric car charging by pulling my car alongside to charge (no, I don't understand her logic either). I didn't shout back. Or try and calm her down. No one ever calmed down by being told to calm down, did they? I just got back in my car, locked the doors, phoned the car charging customer service number and waited until she drove off. Perhaps it's the depleting oestrogen. Or maybe I'm just tired. But I could not be bothered to argue my corner. On the flip side, the stuff I am willing to argue and tussle about is deeper and more meaningful, like inclusion and equality, and woe betide any big boys at the bus stop picking on someone smaller than them. I can see now why so many of the great feminist movements were started by middle-aged women. Having been on this earth for a few decades, pushed out some kids, been through a job or two, and now in our prime, we get angry about the stuff that really matters, and seem to worry less about pissing people off.

What I've come to learn is that conflict is unavoidable and actually pretty bloody necessary. I like to think of it as the sandpaper of human existence. It helps round off the edges, and shapes us into who we are. Although it might feel more comfortable to bury our heads in the sand, by going through it we can learn from it, and how to manage our response to it. I'm not suggesting that you go outside and start a row about the bins with your neighbour, but when things happen there is a simple way of responding to them that I think deserves more credit: forgiveness. This does not mean always being placid or weak, or engaging in passive forgiveness, or giving up on the argument. But a proactive, assertive, controlled and boundary-marking kind of forgiveness. At this point you might be thinking, 'Oh, here she goes, trying to be all high and mighty,' and I would have said exactly the same if I read that a few years ago, but I'm not just saying this because it's in the Bible. It works. Obviously it's not a magic spell that will make all your troubles disappear in a puff of smoke, but having witnessed my fair share of disagreements, it's the next best thing.

Before we get into the good stuff, I'd like to add a note here about a common argument among atheists when it comes to religion and conflict, which may have already crossed your mind. It's a favourite line among non-believers that religion is the cause of all the world's conflict. And if there really is a God, how can they allow so much fighting and bloodshed in their name? It's true that religion might be the hook many aggressors like to hang their disputes on, but it isn't religion that causes the conflict. Humans cause war, it's just that a lot of them use religion as their justification, because it makes them feel noble and not wretched. Making a conflict about how you are favoured by God, and about how God isn't friends with the enemy, justifies your warfare, and makes you feel righteous. Onward Christian soldiers and all that.

Conflict can tear us apart

In my job, you meet more folk who can't forgive than those who can. And who can blame them, it's not something we're really taught after the age of five. Whenever I visit a family before a funeral, I always ask them if there's something they'd like to tell me, by which I mean something they'd like to get off their chest, perhaps about the person who has died and the relationship they had with the deceased. It doesn't matter if there's a mattress or a Maserati on the drive, a fridge or a Ferrari on the front garden, every family has its own story of estrangement and wrongs gone unforgiven.

I'll never forget the story of one family I worked with early on in my vicaring life, while I was still a curate (which is like an apprentice vicar). I was part of the team that looked after a church in a former mining community in north Nottinghamshire. As a community, it wasn't that different to the one I'd grown up in, around Sheffield. They were both post-industrial communities who'd been knocked off their collective feet when the industry that was their beating heart was shut down.

For us in Sheffield it was the manufacturing works. The 'works' was never just a job to the families who worked there: the 'works' provided social clubs, outings to the seaside, football leagues, parties, Easter eggs and everything else in between. They were a whole life, not simply a job. You lived alongside the people you worked alongside. And when the jobs went, so too did people's dignity, self-esteem and sense of purpose. With no jobs there was no money, no shops or services. Everything was shut, only loneliness and depression were left.

Years later there's been some recovery, with the location of businesses like internet-shopping fulfilment warehouses, or sandwich-making factories, providing employment. But the other stuff that supported the workers and their families – the older folk's lunches, the kids' trips to the seaside and the weekend socials – they've never been replaced.

In much of Yorkshire and north Nottinghamshire, the industry was coal mining and the closure of the pits led to many bitter strikes during the 1980s, as miners and their families fought to keep their livelihoods afloat. Many mining communities found themselves opposed to one another, with those who chose to strike and those who chose to continue working in the face of their impending unemployment. In the coalfields and pits of South Yorkshire, miners 'held the line' (went out on strike). But Nottinghamshire was different – there was more of a mixture, with many miners choosing to continue working until their pits were closed. In north Nottingham, you were one or the other, a striker, or what came to be a dirty word: a scab. And scabs and strikers could live next door to each other, or even be in the same family. I was a kid during the strikes, but found myself ministering in these communities almost thirty years later. And although the strikes were now in the past, the deep splits between families and friends that they had caused still ran deep. It's a part of national history that is often retold in films and drama, *Sherwood* being a good example.

In the family that I went to see that day, the split presented itself like an open wound as soon as I walked through the door. I was here to see the family of the man who had died and to talk about the service, and which of his family members would need a mention. You don't want to drop a clanger in the service, so I usually say something like: 'Families are complicated, including mine. Is there something I need to know about your family? Just so I don't put my foot in it?' A couple of things tend to happen at this point: either they say no and I just have to hope that whatever the 'thing' is it stays silent and hidden and I don't say anything too off the mark in the service. Or they say yes, and they open up. This time they opened up.

The wife of the man who had died began to tell the story of their family back in the early 1980s. The man had gone out on strike but his brother hadn't, and the feud that erupted between them as a result had never ended. As the man had lain dying, his brother had visited and tried to make amends with him, but the dying brother had clung to his accusation of 'scab' and rejected him. Now he wasn't welcome at the funeral, either. The family felt the non-striking brother had only tried to make things right at the final hour to ease his own conscience, not because he actually wanted to make amends, but to heal a bruised ego. They didn't want to forgive him even now, in death.

It's never my place to comment on the rights and wrongs of these kinds of disagreements. But this family's story reminded me that forgiveness is not always available on request. And that although it's easy to talk nobly about forgiveness – which we do a lot in the Christian faith – when we are confronted with situations that require us to be forgiving, it's not such a walk in the park. 'Forgive one another as I have forgiven you,' says Jesus. But that's easy for him to say as the son of God, less so for us flawed mortals, right?

It's hard to forgive when someone has hurt or betrayed us. Perhaps because attached to the notion of forgiveness is that there is admission of defeat. That in forgiving someone else we are somehow giving up on our anger and letting them get away with it without suffering the consequences of our anger. But anger can take a lot of physical, mental and spiritual effort. Don't get me wrong, anger is not a bad thing. Channelled and used carefully, anger can right wrongs, facilitate justice and change the world for the better, but anger takes a lot of energy. In situations like the two miner brothers I encountered, anger has grown and cultivated over years. As the anger grows and turns into hatred it gathers stories and experiences around it to justify its existence and feed it. I call this 'I never liked him anyway.' The forgotten birthday gift, the cancelled arrangements, things that have been overlooked for years pop back into the memory and attach themselves to this new trauma, words like 'He always was selfish, remember when . . .' Forgiveness wouldn't just mean forgiving an isolated incident but might mean having to revisit past conflicts and forgive them too.

Anger and resentment are exhausting, but often we'd rather go through that than take the alternative and intimidating route of altering our image. Deciding to forgive someone means that we have to let go of familiar anger which we've made our companion. If I'm the person that had a fall-out with her sister thirty years ago and then we decide to forgive each other and be reconciled, my identity changes. I change who I am to myself, to my sister and to the people around me, and that's scary – who will I be if I am no longer estranged or angry about this?

'Forgive and forget' is another line we hear a lot, although I don't think Jesus said it. When we've been through some sort of conflict with another person we are told that forgiving and forgetting are supposed to go hand in hand. But I'm not so sure about that. If forgetting means not remembering how you've been hurt, and so making yourself vulnerable to the same hurt again next time, I think that's a sort of stupidity. It goes against all our human evolutionary instincts for self-protection and survival. I'm not talking here about holding a grudge – the Bible says, 'Be as wise as a serpent and gentle as a dove'; here wisdom is to forgive and gentleness means ensuring that everything is resolved so that the same thing doesn't happen again.

We are all forgiven

It's an obligation in the Christian faith to forgive. It's a similar situation in many other faiths – forgiveness is one of those biggies that most of the big religions concur on. But there is something about Christianity that, for me, makes it different, and that's the notion of grace. Good deeds are important; we know that doing good makes us feel good. Even those who don't consider themselves to be part of an organized religion usually have a concept of what we send out into the world somehow coming back. Of karma, I guess, and that ultimately those who are 'good people' will be rewarded. For most faiths the concept of doing good things to get into heaven, or the equivalent, is the goal. And there are those of the Christian tradition who talk about that too. I think doing good is good, but I don't think that doing good things alone is going to secure me my place in the hereafter. You see, I'm a mess. We all are. Every single one of us. We all lie, cheat, steal. We kid ourselves that we're not bad people, and most of us aren't, but equally we are none of us perfect. Christians talk a lot about 'Jesus dying for our sins', and although 'sin' is an old-fashioned kind of word, if you think of it as more like being a big old mess like me or you, it takes on new meaning. It means we are loved and forgiven just as we are, even when you lie to your child that there was no cake left (when in fact you'd eaten their slice), or you've accidentally scanned a pomegranate as a lemon on the self-checkout and not corrected it, or even when we do genuinely nasty things. No matter what we do, we are loved by the author of love itself. That blows my mind.

It doesn't mean we shouldn't try to be good – hopefully it's not news that being good is generally the best idea for all involved – but it does mean that even if we don't always manage it, we are loved anyway. There's a pretty massive, overarching responsibility inherent in that concept, which is that, if I'm forgiven and loved, it means everyone else is too. It means we all have to find space to forgive others, even those who've done the most terrible things. But there's also a comfort and a luxury to it – that when we mess up, which we all do, we know it's going to be OK. That, for me, is the essence of Christian grace, and the beauty of forgiveness as an ethos to live by.

But isn't that basically just a big fat get-out-of-jail-free card, I hear you cry? Doesn't that mean that anyone can do anything they like, and we have to just forgive them for it? This is one of the questions I get asked most, especially by people who are struggling to forgive someone who has harmed them or done something, for want of a better word, unforgivable. I sometimes joke, when someone is confessing something 'bad': 'Don't worry, I'm contractually obliged to forgive you anyway.' And I am. But I always think this is where forgiveness becomes really interesting. Because, even though conflict is inevitable, forgiving is often seen as an altruistic act, a way of literally giving relief and freedom to someone else. But I think at its heart, forgiveness is about something much more powerful than being kind. I think forgiveness is a powerful act of self-love and self-preservation. Carrying the pain and resentment of an argument around can get really heavy. Forgiving someone is about setting that load down, taking it off your shoulders. It's about taking back the power in your story and shaping it. You've had something terrible done to you, and forgiveness is your chance to regain control of the story.

Once, a woman came up to me in an art gallery – she said she recognized me from the telly, so I smiled and introduced myself. She responded with the sweetest smile and said, 'I think you are dreadful. Your family must be so ashamed of you.' I'll be honest, at that moment I didn't know whether to cry or punch her. In the end I went to the loo, cried and then went back out there; when she came over to me again I stopped her before she could speak, told her how much what she had said had hurt and how I wasn't prepared to let her do that again. I hoped she had a nice day and I walked away. I often play my other options in that scenario through in my head. The cutting come-back that would have made her feel small. The personal slur and sharp quip that would have put her in her place. She made me cry, after all. But I'm not sure making her cry in return would have been the right thing for either of us. I've no idea if she sometimes still thinks about it like I do, but I know that lashing back at her wouldn't have made anything better – I don't think her misery would have diminished mine. Have I forgiven her? I think so. But every time I retell the story or revisit it in my mind I feel like I have to forgive her all over again, though perhaps not as deeply or painfully. It might be argued it's foolish to rake over old coals to keep thinking about how I was wronged, picking at the wound, but forgiveness is not usually a one-time occurrence. You can't go to one yoga class and call yourself a guru, it takes practice and frequency. I think forgiveness is like that too.

I'm not sure what she thought she was going to achieve by passing on her dislike. Perhaps she didn't think, or perhaps she thought that as a person in the public eye I ought to be able to hear and accept whatever criticism I am given. I'd like to say it's an isolated incident, but it isn't. Usually the conflict I face in public is infrequent and more micro-aggressive, averaging about once a week face-to-face (more online); it's typically a comment on my weight or how my dress didn't suit me on telly the other day. Sometimes I'll gently challenge back fairly passive-aggressively, saying something like, 'Thank you for your comment. I suspect you think you're being kind but I'd rather you didn't say anything,' but, more often than not, I choose not to pick up the comment, to explain it away as rudeness, to smile and to mutter 'idiot' under my breath as I walk away.

When things like this happen and people act so callously towards me, I am reminded of when Jesus says: 'If someone slaps you on the left cheek, turn and offer them the other.' It's something he put into practice during his arrest and trial, when he chose to remain silent in the face of the accusations against him, despite being given the opportunity to save himself. But this defiant silence for me is not a weakness but rather a display of ultimate strength. Louder than any shouting, arguing back doesn't usually change anyone's mind, certainly not on Twitter.

You have to choose your battles, and usually when I'm doing the big shop in Tesco doesn't feel like the time or the place, so I just turn the other cheek. The lady in the art gallery had a big bag of nasty opinions which she wanted to give to me, but I chose not to take them from her. Yes, people will push your buttons, but you don't have to attend every argument you're invited to.

Stand up for yourself

For some people, forgiveness can translate to being a pushover, that being too forgiving is evidence that you somehow lack backbone or strength. But true forgiveness is just as often about seizing back power, particularly when it's a situation where you have been vulnerable or victimized. Forgiveness shifts the power dynamic away from the perpetrator and back to the victim.

Of course, it's not always possible to fix everything. Some stuff stays broken. And no amount of forgiveness, apologies or attempts at reconciliation makes a difference, so it's also wise to know when to walk away. Jesus once said to his disciples, 'If you are not made welcome in a house, shake the dust off your feet and leave.' By which he's saying there's no need to stay, and to try to cajole and persuade others to change, but instead you should assert yourself, take control and leave. This can be interpreted differently, but I've always loved this image of him dusting himself off (the feet were very symbolic back then, so this is kind of the equivalent of sticking your finger up at someone) and marching out with his head held high, refusing to be made to feel unwelcome. A bit like I did with the rude woman in the art gallery. I decided not to try to win her over or find out why she didn't like me so much, but instead stopped her right there and walked away. If forgiveness is taking the moral high ground, that felt like forgiveness to me that day.

When you picture it this way, forgiveness is far less about giving up, denying your anger or pretending dark emotions don't exist. The point of forgiving isn't to achieve a zen-like passivity or to avoid conflict just to live a calm, serene life. It's about reclaiming your personal narrative and standing up for what you believe in, particularly when you have been wronged. Forgiveness is about self-care and standing up for yourself, it's about taking back control of the narrative so that you can decide its terms, path and conclusion. Forgiveness isn't a weakness, it's ultimate strength.

I'd argue that another great example of this from the

Bible is the story of Jesus and the money-lenders. Jesus is often portrayed as meek and mild, passive and compliant, but that's not the Jesus I see. The story goes that on entering the temple Jesus sees that it has become a place almost exclusively for trade rather than worship. There's nothing wrong with trade in itself, but there's money-lenders and tax collectors and other folk of notoriously dubious financial management all hanging out in the temple, which should be a safe space for prayer and contemplation. Most of us remember this story as though Jesus walked in, saw what was going on and started flipping tables in a knee-jerk reaction from a place of furious anger, but the bit I love is where it says, 'he made a whip of cords'. This suggests there was time for Jesus to reflect on what he'd seen and to make the whip of cords, and even by the time he gets back to the temple and starts turning over tables, Jesus was still mad because he and his beliefs had been wronged. Next time you find yourself in a conflict and someone who is trying to promote passivity and gentleness asks, 'What would Jesus do?' remind them that even Jesus lost his rag sometimes. Getting angry and standing up for yourself is human too, and kind of a biblical principle.

When it's not about what it's about

Of course, the worse someone's act, the harder it is to forgive them, particularly if they are a stranger who has committed a crime against us. In our civilized Western culture, forgiveness and mercy are all mixed up with justice and reparation, with bringing fairness to the unfair. Here, forgiving those who trespass against us is about choosing to release ourselves from the story. If someone steals my bicycle when I've popped into the Co-op, it makes me cross, but when I forgive them, they cease to have any power in the narrative. I acknowledge my privilege here, though, and as always my advice comes with a big 'but'. Beyond a broken-into vehicle and a nicked mobile phone, I've never had to forgive someone for a serious criminal offence against me or my loved ones. And I've never met the person who did me wrong. I always find it astounding to read the stories of victims of serious crime who have not only met the perpetrator, but have forgiven them, sometimes even befriended them. These stories tend to get a lot of attention in the news, and rightly so. I'm always tearful when I read them, amazed at the strength of the victim and the power they have.

One of the biggest exercises in forgiveness that is required of me is more modest (and I pray it will remain so) than serious crime. I exercise my forgiveness a lot on social media and the general communication with strangers that comes with being a public figure. I get shouted at a lot by people – online and in person. People want to cheerfully tell me how they think I look prettier in real life, or fatter on telly, or how I'm annoying, or too Northern, or shorter than they thought. There is a general

CONFLICT

assumption that people wouldn't dream of saying the nasty stuff they say online to someone face-to-face, but I'm afraid to say that simply isn't true. I've found there are many people who are just as willing to tell me they hate me up close and personal as they are when they are safely behind their keyboard. Once a man in a Tesco car park called me 'The whore of Babylon'. I wish I'd come up with a witty quip, but instead I phoned my telly vicar mate Richard Coles, who once I'd stopped crying enough to tell him what had happened said: 'Tesco, darling, you poor thing, get to a Waitrose immediately.'

Sometimes it's worse than just a stranger venting at me. I've been threatened with violence and sexual assault, and another time someone told me they hoped my children got cancer. When I tell people this they are often quite shocked, as though being a vicar gives me a special no-abuse pass on Facebook. Unfortunately, every person in the public eye gets abused on social media (and plenty who aren't in the public eye). Most of the time I don't respond to them directly, but that doesn't mean I don't do something. At the moment I've got a regular correspondent who tells me in handwritten letters that I am eternally damned, and assures me with great certainty that my children will meet an early death and those I love will be tortured. Another person told me he was going to come and watch me through my curtains while I got ready for bed at night and wanted to have sex with me on my sofa. I report them to the police, of course, but often they aren't traceable and little can be done. Although I'd like to say it doesn't affect me, I'm only human, and vengeance is something that crosses my mind. I think about what I'd do if left alone with one of these weirdos in a room with no cameras and a baseball bat, of course I do. But of course, the chances are I'd get talking to them and feel desperately sorry for them. Because while their correspondence is in writing, they remain abstract, faceless bad guys, easy to be angry with. Once they become a person with a name, I suspect I'd be inclined to try to help them.

In the absence of retribution via arrest or baseball bat, I have developed other solutions. First, I remind myself that the thing a person is shouting about is not usually what it's about. I had someone shouting at me recently about how ridiculous I was to believe in God, and how if I really did believe in God I should never be sad when someone dies, and they concluded with an aggressive all-capitals 'HEAVEN ISN'T REAL.' A quick search on their profile page showed they'd recently had a big family bereavement. I suspect they weren't angry with me, but more angry with the God they didn't believe in and were perhaps deeply grieving. Happy, contented people don't shout at strangers on the internet, so when someone calls me fat on social media I suspect it's because they feel pretty horrible about themselves. Of course, I don't know what is really going on inside someone's head, not even Derren Brown can do that, but this mantra, 'It's not about what it's about', helps me in those moments.

Next, I pray. First I pray for them, mainly because one of my favourite proverbs from the Bible says that praying for your enemies is like heaping hot coals on their heads. But also because I want to be able to see the human behind their communication. These messages are often not about me but more about the pain and hurt the correspondent feels and the need to project it somewhere. I think sometimes they don't think I see that, so I pray to help them realize the disconnect between what they are feeling and what they are saying. Most of the time I will turn the other cheek and not engage because they are mostly doing it for attention, but occasionally I've picked up communication with them to ask how they are. I know one famous radio friend who used to call back those who sent abusive texts in to their show and ask them for a coffee to discuss their issues more. Cue fierce backtracking by the abuser. There's power in being kind to those who expect you to react with hatred and anger or to ignore them. I find responding to a vile tweet with 'Are you OK?' is a better response than most. Then I pray for myself, not that their words won't affect me, but that if there's any truth in what they say I'll allow it to shape me. The ones that hurt the most are always the ones that have a grit of truth in them. My hope is that the grit of truth can form a pearl. And then of course I forgive them. I have to, otherwise the anger and desire for vengeance would consume me, I'm sure. It doesn't matter to me that they haven't asked for forgiveness, or whether they even think they did something wrong in abusing me, but I have to forgive them to move on (and mute them, of course).

Forgiving yourself

We all have things that make us lie awake at night. I run scenarios from past conflicts over and over in my head, rewriting what I should have said and how I should have reacted. Forgiving ourselves and allowing a line to be drawn under our experience can often be harder than forgiving someone else. Being kind to myself doesn't mean letting myself off the hook. But rather holding myself accountable through honesty.

I see a spiritual director every couple of months – he's a sort of soul friend. Not a trained counsellor or a life coach or even a work consultant but someone with spiritual wisdom who gives me a space to talk while he listens. On the surface this sounds all rather nice and you might be imagining some sort of elderly monk with kind eyes and a whiff of incense. Nothing could be further from the truth. My spiritual director is a nice man and wise, but he isn't always kind. I've been seeing him now for about ten years and we've been through some stuff. These days we know each other so well that we can take the pace a little slower, but when we first started we got to the big stuff really early on.

One of our first sessions was on jealousy. I have a

friend, Anna, who is beautiful, and everything I'm not. She's tall, slim, blonde, pretty, and whenever I go anywhere with Anna people fall over themselves to talk and flirt with her. She's clever and well loved and frankly, I used to hate her. Every time we had to share a space I wished only bad things for her. The patriarchal culture we live in, which so often seems to pit women against each other, didn't help. Neither did it help that Anna was training to be a vicar in the same church as me and that people were constantly comparing us to one another. I decided enough was enough and I should try to do something about the way I felt when I was around her. My spiritual director took me through a confession process where I had to say out loud all the bad things I'd thought and said about Anna, and then he asked me to go and seek her forgiveness. Which I did. Of course she knew we weren't best friends, and that we would often circle each other or be overly nice to one another to mask how we really felt. But I think asking for her forgiveness for being so unkind about her behind her back was a really powerful thing to do. It strengthened our relationship with one another and made me feel like a stronger, better person. It wasn't a one-time event though, it's an action I have to practise and repeat. I know I have a problem with jealousy and other women. I'm not sure it's something I'll ever fully conquer. I've unfollowed and lost contact with friends over it, simply because of the person I become when they are around. I find it especially difficult when I see their children being highly successful, or if they achieve massive weight-loss or meet fitness goals. Jealousy is an ugly beast and I don't like the person I am when I feel it. I don't know what the answer is, or whether this is just a battle that I will never fully overcome. But I do know that confession, saying things out loud, absolution and forgiveness are the key to not necessarily killing my jealousy dragon, but certainly getting it on a lead and teaching it to behave. Even just writing about it here and sharing this with you has tamed it a little more.

Church of England folk don't always go in for formal confession, you know like you see in *Fleabag* where the person goes into a little cupboard with a priest on the other side. But we do have it as a thing, though it's more like a chat these days. And you can ask for it to be anonymous if you wish. It's basically a bit like going to the dentist. I don't go for ages, and then once I've been I wonder why I left it so long and what on earth the fuss was about. My confessor asks tough questions, makes me feel uncomfortable, leaves just enough silence for me to fill the void with my own words. I usually cry, that's OK. I try to make excuses, that isn't. But I always leave with a job to do, an action. It's cathartic to draw a line under the things that I'm beating myself up about but, just like our trips to the dentist, the job is never finished. We are only human and it is inevitable that we do things that we feel guilty about, so it is only natural that we keep on saying sorry, seeking reconciliation and enjoying the post-forgiveness glow. Forgiveness of ourselves and others is a practice that needs constant work. The good news is that it does get easier and more instinctive over time.

I know that for many people, therapy and counselling provide the same sort of release. And much like being religious, there is a certain taboo around 'needing' therapy. People don't always like to say if they are having counselling. And I wonder why that is. Somewhere along the way we seem to have lost the skill for seeking forgiveness, and forgiving ourselves. Perhaps this is what the 'self-care' movement is really about. A need to fill the void where once we acknowledged our failures, said sorry and moved on. All I know is that the world would be a better place if we could all forgive ourselves for the things that we are hung up on, to shed that weight pulling us down. Imagine how much more energy we'd have to put into other things. Carrying all those grudges and resentments and all that self-loathing can be exhausting. Like the old Buckaroo donkey, if we keep taking on those burdens we will eventually lose ourselves completely. Think of the way that Archbishop Desmond Tutu led the truth and reconciliation conversations after the fall of apartheid in South Africa. He could do this because of his faith and his belief about the important and tough work of forgiveness. Even though it's considered to be a divine gift, forgiveness isn't a magical power, it's a skill that can be developed and it isn't exclusively owned by the religious – so go ahead, help yourself.

THREE GOOD THINGS

Like all the subjects in this book, forgiveness is not a destination or a skill to be developed or acquired somehow. It's a process, one that continues to progress, regress, revisit, change and shape over time. Try these three things to keep your forgiveness muscles in shape:

1. **Take a breath.**
   Next time you find yourself in a conflict situation, whether it's a complaint to the phone company or a row with your teenage child, try a new tactic. One of the most powerful things you can do in a conflict is to absent yourself and give yourself time before forming your response. Rarely does a knee-jerk response from anger end well. And you may say too much or too little, which you'll grow to regret. You cannot manage anyone else's response, but you can manage your own. Start by stepping away from the conflict. This isn't about avoiding discussions, more about coming back to them when you are calm and have had time to let things settle.

2. **Make amends.**
   Using the model of confession, forgiveness, reconciliation, perhaps there is a situation unresolved with someone that you might be able to work through. Is there an old friend you feel you treated badly and would like to ask for

forgiveness? Or has someone betrayed you and you're keen to find a way to forgive them? How might you move this forward? Would some counselling or confession help?

3. **Absolve yourself.**
You don't have to go to confession to get that forgiveness buzz – it comes from within. Write down those things you feel sorry for, mistakes, errors of judgement, times you messed up – you could write them on a piece of paper and burn it, or on a wipe-clean board, or on a stone and throw it into running water. When you see the writing disappear from the stone and get washed away, allow yourself to feel absolved and rejoice.

5. Confidence

As we go through life, another crisis that we're likely to come up against is that of confidence. Like all the topics in this book, this will look different for different people, but I'd say the biggies are mainly our appearance, career and relationships, not necessarily in that order. Some people seem to have it in truckloads, others seem incapable of ever finding enough of it to do the things they want to do in life. I guess that's what confidence is, it's the fuel to power you through the challenges that come so thick and fast in life, whatever they may be.

For me, especially because of the work I do, confidence is inextricably linked to being in the public eye, to standing up in front of an audience or getting in front of a camera. You'd imagine that doing these things on a regular basis might require a level of pre-existing confidence in my own abilities, or I might at least have cultivated it over the years. You don't get up there to deliver the news that Jesus is Lord to a crowd of non-believers without feeling at least slightly OK about the exposure that comes with this kind of public appearance. It's true that these days my confidence seems to slowly be growing and that, I think, is probably something to do with my age. Ask an old person and they'll tell you that the older you get the less bothered you are by daunting tasks and situations, because you have lived through enough of them to know that you usually come out of the other side alive. But it hasn't always been this way for me, and it often comes as a shock to people when I say I wasn't always as confident as I am now.

As a little girl I was painfully shy and would hide behind my mum's legs when we stopped to chat to people in the street. I got my first taste of confidence when I was very small, on holiday in Spain. The kind of holidays we went on in my family had those clubs that the kids could go to while the parents relaxed and enjoyed a beer beside the pool. Me and my brother would be packed off to the kids' club for the day and, to my glee (yes, my competitive streak started early), they had regular competitions. One of those competitions was a talent contest and, despite my lack of confidence to speak in front of adults, I wanted so badly to enter it. I think I was only about five, so I don't remember much, but I put my name on the list and prepared the nursery rhyme I wanted to sing. I remember it was a busy, hot, crowded room – I suppose it must have been the place where the evening entertainment happened, repurposed for the kids' talent show. I also remember, I guess because I was so small, lots of legs. As I walked on to the stage, I remember realizing that the room was packed. I don't remember what I sang, what I was wearing or how I sounded, but I do remember the feeling of being nervous but excited as I performed, and then, the applause.

Yep, that's right, as you may have guessed (considering that I'm choosing to tell you this story), I won! Having beaten my teenage competitors, my prize, a sombrero, was for a much older child and was far too big for me, but I pulled it on to my head with pride. I ran down the beach towards my dad clinging on to this sombrero for dear life, shouting at the top of my voice, 'Daddy, Daddy, I won! I won!' More than forty years later my dad can't tell that story without crying. The feeling of winning, the sound of the applause and the pride of my dad meant those first seeds of confidence (or being a show-off, depending how you look at it) were sown.

Now I don't know if it's to do with gender, or class, or parental expectations, but 'showing off' was always something seen as a bad trait. Yes, my family have always been proud of me, and that sombrero was the catalyst for it all, but I've always been aware of other people's opinions. At times I've felt that I've been treading a fine line between being a happy entertainer and being an 'attention seeker'. I'm not sure I always got it right, and I'm still not.

It doesn't mean that some of my relatives didn't like the spotlight themselves, though. I come from a large extended family and we are all pretty outgoing – it was fairly usual for people to get up at family parties and do their turn. My mum and dad could dance, I mean really dance, especially my dad. At any given wedding recep-tion there'd be a discreet request for 'Jailhouse Rock', and Margaret and Arthur would take to the floor. Then my auntie Mary would ask for Tina Turner and she'd get up and dance on the table flashing her stocking tops. Any time the aunties and uncles went on a big night out for New Year's Eve, they'd all go in fancy dress. A dozen of them togged up as Morris dancers, monopolizing the high street, fuelled by beer and having a blast.

A contradiction

Once I hit puberty, my propensity for performing went stratospheric. A stint at a local youth theatre, a part in a play on Radio 4 and a role in an ITV drama (I was in *The Life and Times of Henry Pratt*, playing Betty Bridger opposite a very young Johnny Lee Miller. If you want to see my earnest performance, over-egging as best I could, you can look it up on YouTube). I'm not saying this to blow my own trumpet, quite the opposite. Yes, I'm more than happy to talk to huge numbers of people, to be on the telly and radio and to work a room full of vicars or telly people or both. I delight in fancy dress and almost any kind of being looked at (with my consent – I don't mean I enjoy being watched by stalkers), but even my confidence has its cracks. There is the other side of me that no one except for my family sees: I find it almost impossible to book appointments over the phone, and talking on the phone in general, to be honest. I find it toe-curlingly embarrassing, and I think I sound really stupid. My answerphone message on my mobile says, 'I don't answer my phone, please text or email.' That isn't because I'm so busy, I just would really rather not go through the torment of a phone conversation and all the potential mini-disasters it represents. Similarly, I never answer the door at home. I can't bear ordering takeaway deliveries, because it means someone coming to the house (something I had to get over quickly when the *Gogglebox* film crew descended on our house twice a week for three years!) and they might judge me for eating junk food, or catch a glimpse of the mess in my hallway, or expect a tip when I haven't got any cash. They might see me without any make-up on. They might see the real me! Bonkers, isn't it? Even when I'm at work, before a funeral visit, I sit in the car for a few minutes to talk myself into it, not because I don't want to talk about death, but because I struggle to find the confidence to knock on the door and introduce myself to these griev-ing people. What if they don't like me? What if I can't do the job? As if in their bereavement it's my ego that matters. Imposter syndrome isn't only for people in cor-porate jobs, vicars get it too you know. I know it's talked about a lot these days, but I think it's always a helpful reminder that no matter how much others seem to have everything sussed on the outside, there is always so much more going on beneath the surface. We're all in the same boat.

My trick when I get nervous, or feel the self-doubt creeping in, is to give myself a talking to. I start by listing all the things I have achieved in the past. I start with:

'You are a confident, capable, articulate woman. There are little girls who want to be like you when they grow up.' (Now I haven't had any little girls actually say that, but there have been a few grown-ups who've told me that when they were exploring their own vocation they were grateful that I seemed to make the whole thing look like it might be possible to do without entirely losing all trace of personality – so, near enough.) And I take it from there: exams, the birth of my kids, my work, anything I can think of that will help, doing an audit of my achievements to tell myself I'm better and stronger than I think.

My talks-to-self don't always work, but I've definitely surprised myself over the years with how, even if my efforts have failed in the short term, I've somehow managed to grow through sheer determination. It might sound ridiculous, but as part of my vicar training I had a go at stand-up comedy, fire-eating and magic tricks, so as to build my confidence in front of a crowd and so I'd have a virtual goody bag of talents when it came to doing school assemblies. I'll never forget the fear in a headteacher's face when as a curate I whipped out my fire-eating equipment in a school assembly, although they did book me for the summer fayre. More recently I was challenged to learn Welsh for a TV programme I was recording (the weirdest jobs are always for TV programmes) and I gladly took it on, because I work with a lot of Welsh people and I felt guilty that I could say 'hello' in most European languages, but not in the home language of Welsh. It was tough and made me cry more than once, and trying to find the confidence to speak any Welsh in public took a long time. It sounds silly, but losing face, being bad at something, took every ounce of my confidence and really necessitated putting my big girl pants on. But, regardless of how much I've achieved, the brilliant news is: I am still a work in progress, constantly changing and developing. I know people are just being kind when they say, 'You're so great, never change!' but I think it's such a nonsense and always respond, 'I hope I bloody will!' I've come to believe that when you stop trying at things, even if you suspect you might fail, that's when your confidence really withers. Not in the failing, but in the failing to try. It's never too late to try something new or try something again. I love the line: change is life.

There is certainly a lot of mileage in the old adage, 'Fake it till you make it', but ultimately, no one can pretend to be something they're not for very long, and you shouldn't feel any pressure to be something you are not. I think true confidence goes hand in hand with authenticity. I felt like an idiot at times when I was learning Welsh, but I was doing it for a good reason, and for me. That's the key, I think: making sure that you are striving to achieve things for you, and not to impress someone else or do what you think society wants you to do. This can be especially true for us girls, whom society, and our bodies, seem to have plans for long before we know about them. Homemaker and wife, mother and carer – these roles seem to be reserved only for us. I don't think it's a coincidence that confidence, or lack of, seems to affect the women I meet more than the men. I'm not saying men have an easier time of things – God knows they have their own challenges to face. But I am saying that pretty much all the women I know are always doing things for other people. And they are often the ones who struggle with their confidence, and there is something to think about in that.

On body confidence

The Bible calls the body 'a temple for the holy spirit'. While our spirit and what that means might differ wildly from human to human, our bodies are the one thing we all have in common. They are the physical representation of our minds, where all our memories and experiences are stored and processed. The vessels in which our spirits are held.

It's fair to say that I use my body more than most people, and I do a lot of work for the divine – but it's still not easy for me to remain holier than thou about it all. Western society is built on values that cause people to be judged on their weight and the space they take up in the world, and this, my friends, is something I have always struggled with. You might think that because I'm a vicar I don't or shouldn't care about my appearance. But just like everyone else, my confidence is affected by the rhetoric around body image. And despite the fact that you can often see me prancing around in my swimming costume on social media, I am not at peace with my body.

I know that logically speaking, it is ridiculous to think this way; for one thing, I know that most of the time, most of us are far too concerned with ourselves to worry about what anyone else looks like. In the grand scheme of things, it's only a few very sad and angry individuals on social media who seem to feel the need to care deeply about the size and shape of someone else's body. I can usually remember this and feel empowered in my own skin – I call it getting into Lizzo mode. Wonderful, beautiful, big-bottomed Lizzo.

And yet. I still have days when I hate my body. I've always hated it. It sounds a bit strong for a vicar, doesn't it? Someone who should be at peace with herself and not be concerned with such superficial things as the body and how she looks. But it's true. There's a Psalm that says: 'You are fearfully and wonderfully made.' In an ideal world we'd all embrace this sentiment and all feel wonderfully wonderful about the way we are put together – wouldn't we? But like a lot of us, I find I am often more focused on the fearful bit, the voice that tells me I'm not good enough. Too round, too fat, too short.

We live in a culture that tells us we are faulty from the moment we are born. Very early on in life I came to understand that thinness was to be prized above almost everything else, and that I was not thin. I remember taking part in dancing competitions as a six-year-old, and being told my dress would fall nicer if I just held my tummy in. At junior school in PE lessons, I experienced my first episode of what we now call fat-shaming. One of the girls in my class had us all counting our rolls of fat in the changing room – I had the most. I got my first stretch marks when I was about nine years old and noticed my first cellulite not long after. My pale skin scars easily, and by the time I went to university, my tummy, boobs and upper arms looked like they'd been etched with the tributaries of a river. I remember snogging a guy in a bar – he glanced down at my cleavage and said, 'What are all those lines on your tits?' I went to the toilet and cried. (Now, after two babies, my stretch marks go from the top of my boobs all the way down to the tops of my thighs and even my pubis is criss-crossed with stripes. I know, I know, they're normal, but I hate them and avoid mirrors when I'm even slightly naked.) After Ruby, my emergency C-section baby, was born, the midwife wrote on my notes, 'Stomach large and overhanging, difficult to examine.' I think about those words a lot. In fact, one of the churches I was in while I was a curate (apprentice vicar) even had a weight-loss group based on the idea that Jesus wants us skinny, called 'Slim for Him'.

In what feels like a lifelong attempt to change the shape of me, I've been on every diet and weight-loss programme going. Weight Watchers, Slimming World, Cambridge Diet, Cabbage Soup. I've taken laxatives and

I've exercised obsessively. I've kept weight-loss diaries and chewed my food and spat it out. I've sprayed my leftovers with washing-up liquid so that I couldn't finish them. I've eaten less than 800 calories a day, fasted for days at a time and drunk an array of disgusting diet shakes.

My work takes me away a lot these days, and I still find I worry when I order room service in the hotel. I feel like everyone is judging me for my choices: 'She's eating chips! The fat cow in room 47!' My rational brain tells me that no one gives two hoots about what I'm eating, but the monkey on my shoulder tells me otherwise. And as a now-officially-middle-aged woman, it's only getting worse. My depleting oestrogen levels mean I can't seem to lose weight any more, and some days it just seems like I'm getting fatter and fatter and fatter. I might seem like a show-off on social media, and there's no denying I'm happy to be in a career that requires me to be in front of either a crowd, or a camera, or both. But the truth is I don't watch myself back on telly because I can't bear how I look. On photo-shoots for work I often cry, because of how insecure I feel. One photographer even brought her dog along to help me find my confidence in between takes. I can now recommend taking dogs to all photo-shoots.

I have attempted to exorcise my body confidence demons, and as you might expect if you know much about me, I haven't done it half-heartedly. I had a friend do a naked photo-shoot of me back when Gok Wan was

doing his best to encourage all to embrace our bountiful
bangers. I had fun, but I never showed anyone the pictures. I have also been a life drawing model a couple of
times. The first request came into my inbox via my agent,
asking if I'd like to take part in *Life Drawing Live!* I must
have been in an amiable mood that day because I said
yes straight away. My enthusiasm was somewhat diminished when a few weeks later I found myself in the back
of a cab heading towards a public park in the centre of
Birmingham. As families picnicked and played, I sat
draped only in a piece of blue chiffon on a chaise-longue
with my bountiful blessings out. An artist chum of mine
reassured me once that art students much prefer something worth getting their pencil round. I'd like to tell you
it made me feel confident and beautiful but it didn't, it
just made me feel a bit chilly and like I wished I'd thought
to get a spray tan. The second time I was a life model
was during lockdown in 2020, and a little more bizarre.
For context, we all did slightly odd and out of character
things in those unprecedented times: maybe you made
banana bread, I got my tits out for a stranger on a web-
cam. (It's not as dodgy as it sounds, I promise!) A friend
was commissioning an artwork to be auctioned off for
charity: the theme was the garden of Eden and they
needed an Eve, would I pose? Of course we wouldn't be
able to do the sitting in person, because not only did
Covid prevent our contact, but the artist was based in
Italy. So I warned Kev next door not to look over the
fence, propped my laptop up on the wheelie bin and got

naked in my garden (the light was better than inside) in the middle of the day while a man I'd only met online took some photos. We got on like a house on fire, so much so that he asked to paint me again. I posed a couple more times, and when the paintings were finished he asked me if I'd like to buy them. I didn't have the 8k loose change so I declined. I do know who did buy one though. And that's how a naked picture of me hangs on the guest bedroom wall of Bear Grylls's sister's house.

What's interesting, though, is that losing weight doesn't solve the problem. There have been times when I've lost a lot of weight and ironically I've hated it when people commented on it. I hate the attention weight loss brings. There's a kind of public ownership to your body when you're not thin. People telling me I look lovely, or my pet hate 'well', because I'm thinner, simply makes me think they thought I looked hideous before. So I was right all along! The truth is we can't know why a person has lost a lot of weight. When my mum was in intensive care and not expected to survive I lost a huge amount of weight. I stopped eating and consequently people stopped me in the street to tell me how marvellous I looked. The times I've been at my thinnest have almost exclusively been the times when my mental health has been at its worst. To repeat one of my favourite sayings again: 'It's not about what it's about.' Over the years I've come to realize that losing weight isn't what it's about – feeling content with who I am is the real work for me.

I am disappointed in myself for all these feelings. I'm

a person of faith, how my body looks is meant to be immaterial – I'm supposed to be concerned about more important things than my wobbly arse. I'm supposed to simply rejoice in all the amazing and wonderful things my body can do. I'll get to that bit, I will. But I wanted to be honest here, about the way I see my body and the weight – pun intended – that I carry around in this small and sturdy frame of mine. Because I know that the way I feel is not that unusual, especially for women. Even as a vicar, I am not impervious to the relentless body/ woman/fat-shaming our culture promotes. And then, of course, not only do I feel like a terribly shallow person, a dreadful role model and a terrible feminist, but I also feel guilty about feeling ashamed of my body. It's exhausting.

A gift

Someone said on social media somewhere that, 'The opposite of sad is not happy, it's gratitude', or something like it, and I think they're right. Despite the fact that I go around saying I hate my body, I am also simultaneously completely grateful for my body and all the things it lets me do. (I'm a big fan of allowing ourselves to feel seemingly contradictory things at the same time – love and anger, capable but struggling, proud but anxious – you get the idea.) A spiritual friend of mine sometimes does a meditation with me, called a gratitude body scan, where we both lie there on the floor in her living room and go from the very top of our heads (including hair) down to our toes via every muscle, limb and organ in between, and think about how grateful we are to have our bodies, and what they allow us to do.

We should all remind ourselves more often how amazing we are, simply to be alive. I try to remember all the positive experiences my body has given me – the amazing meals I've eaten and the delicious sleepy lie-ins I've had, the nights out dancing and the belly laughs. Our bodies are truly a gift – they enable us to connect with other humans, eat, move, have sex, and enjoy all kinds of spiritual experiences – whether that is swimming in waterfalls and watching the sun rise, meditating, praying, or whatever it is you like to do.

When I'm feeling down about my own body I try to remember these times, when it has served me so well. Once, I did three triathlons back-to-back for Sport Relief and raised a million pounds. The organizers insisted we wore a wetsuit for the swimming challenge and I cried when I had to have mine custom-made. Before being measured for it I drank half a bottle of wine for courage, and insisted the friends that measured me hid the piece of paper they wrote on afterwards. But as I crossed the finish line in last place on the final race for the final time, red in the face and sweating, I marvelled at my amazing body and its ability to do incredible things.

Oh, and of course there was also that time I grew two

babies inside me and gave birth to them. Although at the time of their births, especially Ruby's, I felt my body had let me down. Both my kids were born by Caesarean section – emergency the first time, routine the second – and for a long time I struggled with how somehow my body hadn't been able to do what it was supposed to do: give birth 'naturally'. My pregnancies came at a strange time in my life when I felt I was at the intersection of working-class culture, Northern matriarchs (my family) and the new breed of so-called yummy-mummies, who seemed to be the women wearing Boden whom I met at ante-natal classes and NCT sales. While they couldn't have been more different in their outlook, everyone seemed to agree that childbirth should be as natural as possible and that pain relief and other medical interventions were to be avoided at all costs. All of which told me that needing them was a kind of failure. In fact, for a long time there was a school of religious thought that birth pains were punishment because of Eve's disobedience and should be suffered; as a result, the patriarchy held back the use of anaesthetic for labouring women and it wasn't until Queen Victoria had a tug on some chloroform that it became acceptable. But my babies decided they weren't going to take the usual route out, so I had all the pain relief and the biggest intervention possible. Even though this was the right decision to deliver my babies safely, I struggled with that fact for a long time. I cried about it a lot.

We are all slightly unhinged after childbirth, aren't we?

But dark thoughts troubled me: I wondered if I would be allowed to keep Ruby, because I hadn't pushed her out properly. Isn't that sad? I know that a lot of mums who find breastfeeding difficult and have to bottle-feed are also tormented by these thoughts of being less-than, not a 'natural' mother. Time, the great healer, even better than Sudocrem, and hindsight, have helped me come to see that I was not a failure, but was myself failed by the unrealistic expectations of those around me and the tired conversation about motherhood and what is 'right' and 'wrong'. I argue that there is in fact nothing natural about trying to push a melon-sized human out through a lemon-sized hole, and while it felt painful at the time – emotionally and physically – carrying those two children and bringing them into the world remains my proudest achievement, and balls to anyone who says I was 'too posh to push' or worse, tries to commiserate with me. People say childbirth has become too medicalized these days, but I gently remind them it's called a Caesarean section. It's literally named after the Roman emperor, Julius Caesar, who according to some was born this way, too. It has taken some time but I no longer feel ashamed or let down by my body, and instead I simply feel gratitude for how it got us all safely through that process.

Getting to know people who can't use their bodies in the same way as most of us do, or as well as they used to be able to, has also taught me a lot. One of the staples of being a vicar is visiting people at home. At first I wasn't very good at it, I never knew what to say – we weren't taught this at vicar school and the Bible isn't exactly full of conversation starters – especially to people with dementia in nursing and care homes, or to the dying in hospices. But I quickly learned that there are two important things to remember. First, like I talked about earlier, there is no need to fill the silence – allow the silence to happen. If nothing is being said, that usually means nothing needs to be said and the person you are with might need the space to process what's happening and why you are there. I also learned about the importance of keeping my eyes open, watching what is happening around me. When there is a time for talking and noise, it's often grounded in nostalgia. Music is always good and there's a gift in seeing people move their bodies. The days of jiving might be over, but there's a beauty in watching older people move and enjoy rhythm. Sometimes it might be standing with a frame, or waving arms or even just a nodding head, but to keep moving as much as possible for the health of body, mind and soul is life. And it strikes me that not one of these people I encounter in those kinds of places hates their body in the same way I do. They might hate it because it can't do what it used to, which always serves as a humbling reminder to do what I can while I can.

I know too that hating my body is bad for my health. Back when I was a curate I was struggling with my health. I woke up every day with a pain in my chest and a tight throat; it felt like there was a lump, so I went to see my doctor. Before I'd properly had a chance to explain, he asked me to stand on the scales and talked to me about my weight. I wasn't there about my weight. Eventually he sent me for a blood test, but I never went back for the results. I was afraid he was going to talk about my weight again. This wasn't an isolated incident either. Ear infection? Let's have a conversation about your weight. Contraception? We'll need a conversation about your weight first. Repeat prescription? You guessed it. It didn't matter that all my statistics apart from my BMI were fine, I regularly exercised and I ate good, home-cooked food, but every time I talked about my health the conversation came back to weight. I stopped going to see doctors altogether. Even in worrying moments, when I found a lump on my labia and a mole started to spread, I refused to go and see a doctor. I worked myself into a frenzy of self-loathing. I arranged for a coffee with a friend who is a GP, to talk to her, and heard myself saying at one point: 'If I live to fifty that will be fine.' It seemed reasonable, both kids would be grown up by then and wouldn't need me. There would still be enough time for Graham to find someone else. I didn't find it a shocking sentence to say, I still don't: so difficult was the doctor's constant nit-picking about my weight that I'd decided the damage to my mental health was greater than the risk to my physical health. The worry and anxiety that comes with hating your own body cannot be underestimated. Your body is you, so when you say you hate your legs or your arms or whatever it is you

hate, you're really saying you hate yourself. And if you
hate yourself you don't look after yourself, even when
there are worrying lumps and moles that really need to
be looked at.

It was doing the triathlons that finally changed things
for me. I needed a medical to cover the insurance so that
I could take part. This meant a trip to the doctor. I rang
the surgery in tears to speak to a nurse. I explained I
hadn't been to the doctor in years, that I had lumps and
dodgy moles and I was pretty sure I was really ill, and
also that I was fat. That standing on a scale and being
judged was so terrifying that I was willing to risk my life
to avoid it. She made me a double appointment so we
could have some time together, she told me to text her
when I was in the surgery car park and she would come
outside to meet me and walk me in. She let me bring a
friend. She took everything very slowly. I got there. I had
the tests. I waited. And when the results came in I was
fine, just a bit fat. Even the lumps they weren't concerned about and the dodgy moles. I was and am, and
probably always will be, just a bit fat.

I'm telling you all of this to show that I have mixed
feelings about my body, like everyone does. I'm human.
Being religious, being a Christian who believes I am a
created being with a godly purpose, doesn't mean I am
above the pressure of vanity and appearance; gluttony is
after all considered one of the 'deadly sins' in the Christian tradition, but what can I say? One Hobnob is never
enough, and if there isn't cheese in heaven I'll go to the

other place, I think. So, while I can talk the talk about how much my body has brought me and that we should all be grateful for that, I haven't nailed it yet, and you are not alone in feeling the same way.

Of course, body confidence is my thing. You might have a different thing, when it comes to feeling confident. Maybe you're incredibly shy and lack the confidence to meet new people, which holds you back in relationships and work and going on dates. Maybe you're not sure you're good enough at your job and lie awake at night worrying about what Gary in marketing thinks about you, or you hate your teeth and find it awkward to smile. Maybe you're just worried about the planet and don't have much confidence in the people who are supposed to be saving it. The point is that everyone struggles with confidence at some point, somehow. It's part of being human. And anyone who says they feel 100 per cent confident, 100 per cent of the time, is lying.

Fake it till you make it

That said, there is something in faking it (your confidence, that is . . . we're not going *there*, don't worry). For example, body acceptance is a muscle (pun definitely intended) that I need to exercise every day. That's why, if you follow me on social media, you'll know I'm often posting pictures of myself in a barrel of cold water or swimming in a river – boobs and bum on show for all to see. After my Sport Relief triathlon I posted a picture of my belly overhang. It might look like I'm someone who loves my body and feels confident sharing images of it, but in truth I'm just trying to love it. Every. Single. Day. Only by getting out there and celebrating my body with all its curves and crevices can I find these moments of joy and acceptance. I guess I'm hoping that if I do it enough, one day I will eventually come to love it in the way I know I should. Sometimes having faith can feel the same way – you cling to the rituals and the cere- monies and the sermons, keep putting them out there, even on those days when you're not sure why.

I swim naked and wild from time to time and have found a sense of personal acceptance in that space. I did the North East Skinny Dip in 2019. Seven hundred naked humans on a beach by the North Sea. The night before, we all camped together in the surrounding fields, and there was a campfire and singing. At dawn the next morning, fire dancers and drummers greeted us, and then with a rallying cry from the organizers we all de- robed and made our way to the freezing cold waters. In front of me was a woman with the most amazing huge rolls of back fat I've ever seen, glorious rolls of flesh that reminded me of a painting of a landscape or the rolling hills of the Yorkshire Dales – she took my breath away. The irony was not lost on me, that what I see as beautiful in others, I can struggle to see as beautiful in myself. Or at least, I can't sustain that thinking for long. Just like everyone else I need to give myself regular reminders, like hopping in the barrel, hugging my kids or swimming in a lake, that I appreciate the body that I inhabit.

Wild swimming or bobbing in a barrel isn't only about my body image and the nice pictures for Instagram, either. There is something about the cold temperature that helps me. My coldest ever swim was about minus two degrees, in February, surrounded by the snow-covered moors of the Derbyshire countryside. As dog walkers and ramblers trudged past in balaclavas and mittens, I stripped off to my costume and smashed ice with a sledgehammer in an attempt to feel invincible. It worked, and I keep going back. Yes, the water carries my weight. I don't feel heavy or short in the water. But running and rushing water also has the ability to carry away worries. I also litter-pick when I swim, or womble as we call it. Finding bottles and cans, old sinks and bikes and the ubiquitous shopping trolleys and cones. I'm reminded that the rubbish I pull out of the river is nothing compared to the emotional rubbish the river can wash away. It's all in the breath. Deep and slow, feeling the heart rate rising and the panic as the cold water reaches my thighs and then over my tummy. Feeling that panic and then telling myself to breathe and slow down.

Most extreme sports (and cold water swimming is extreme) are all about aggression, attacking the thing that scares you, pretending it's not scary and painful. But I'd argue that dipping into ice water is about something entirely opposite to that. It's about observing that this is hard, it hurts. Every part of my body is telling me not to go there, but I can dig deep and talk myself down. Rather than attacking the thing that scares you, it's about observing that it's hard and doing it anyway. Proving to yourself in a matter of seconds that you can do hard things. It changes you, it helps you grow. It has meant that when I find myself panicking in other places and situations that are as hostile and as scary as minus two degrees, my brain somehow has a kind of muscle memory that helps me to control my breathing and calm down. It helps.

It's hardly surprising the water helps me – human beings are made up of mostly water, after all – but before the invention of the mirror, which I am so critical about seeing myself in, the only place human beings could go to see themselves was the water. The only way our ancestors could know what they looked like was to look at their reflection in a still pool. For me, it's in water that I see my true self, and feel happy with what I see.

Older and wiser

As I mentioned earlier, every few weeks I see a spiritual director. We vicars get spiritual directors as part of the package. I've been seeing mine for about ten years. The idea is that the spiritual director is a kind of soul friend, someone to help you work through what's going on in your spiritual life. You might call yours a therapist, or just a really good friend. I talk to mine about all sorts of things.

I've been doing some work recently with him about my identity as a woman coming to the end of my oestrogen years. Changes have started happening in my body. I can't seem to string a sentence together, I can't remember anything, I'm gaining weight without even trying (I only glanced at a crumpet a few minutes ago and popped a button on my waistband), and my periods are very much hit-and-miss in their frequency. I've always been susceptible to unscheduled fits of sobbing and anger and it is only getting worse. But what I've found really helpful is looking at other 'wise women', as I like to call them. These are women who have, essentially, reached the stage in their lives where, to put it bluntly, they are no longer fertile. I know logically that women have worth beyond our reproductive capacity, but it feels like once those years are past (whether we were able, chose not to, or did have children) society expects us to find a new role. So I've been looking at some women, roughly fifty and over, whom I admire, famous and not famous, including *the* Judi Dench, Dawn French, my kick-ass neighbour Dianne, my swim sisters Heather and Sarah. I've found it useful to focus on the confidence exuding from these women who have also passed this turning point in life, so that I too can embrace exactly who I am and where I am. My hope is that one day I might also be able to step into the role as someone who can mentor and help other women realize their greatness. Years ago I'd probably have been burnt for being a witch. A spiritual woman with an opinion, who has a wildness and independence of spirit. But not now. Hopefully now I can help people embrace that wildness and show that it can exist alongside faith.

I still have to work on all aspects of my confidence, spiritual, mental and physical, and it feels like that work is going to be lifelong. I have an ambition to be the older lady you see dressed entirely in pink, with three dogs in her wheelie trolley, giving zero fudges about what anyone thinks of her. I have a way to go just yet, but I know that practising through things that make me feel strong and confident, like swimming in freezing temperatures, learning languages and bobbing in a barrel, might just help me get a little closer to achieving this.

THREE GOOD THINGS

No one feels confident 100 per cent of the time and they're probably lying if they say they do. The key is to develop some tools that help boost you and build your confidence in yourself so that you can live the life YOU want to live, regardless of what anyone else thinks. Channel your inner menopausal woman (because I really believe zero oestrogen = zero f*cks), and try these three little things to get you on your way:

1. **Do a confidence audit.**
   List your achievements and talk yourself up. If you don't believe you're amazing, how will anyone else? This is not an exercise in vanity but a way to remind yourself what you've achieved

and what you are capable of. Leave no stone unturned – even if you think it's something that is just 'a given', you did it, so you deserve to bathe in that glory.

2. **Change your screensaver.**

   If body confidence is your Achilles heel, find images of bodies that look like yours, that paint them in a positive light. These might be classical images or more modern photographs (the mid- and plus-size models are coming through more and more, and it's great). Fill your Instagram feed with them, stick their pictures up on your walls, look at the images regularly to counterbalance the images you see of bodies that don't look like yours. I have a collage of Rubensesque bottoms as my screensaver. If it's not about your body but something else, you can still apply this technique to whatever your issue is.

3. **Use Lent to build your confidence in something.**

   I try every now and again to do something a bit different for Lent, as there's only so many times I'm willing to give up chocolate and alcohol. One year I committed to try and introduce myself to forty new strangers, one each day of Lent (Sundays off, of course – did you know you get Sundays off in Lent? You're welcome). I wanted to exercise my confidence muscle, as well as hopefully have some lovely conversations and meet some new people. I was inspired by those street photographers that you see on Instagram. Every time I tried it I went through the cycle of internal pep talk, execution of the challenge and then self-reward. Write yourself your own pep talk, or record it on to your voice notes. Follow it with a congratulations speech. Every time you try something that requires confidence, go through the cycle of pep talk, task, congratulations and reward.

6. Loneliness

I was telling my kids recently about how when I was growing up you used to have to make an appointment to phone your friends. There was no texting, no Whats-App, no Snapchat. Some of my chums didn't even have a phone in their house and had to use the pay phone at the end of the street. I'm not trying to sound like *Monty Python*'s Four Yorkshiremen here, I'm just illustrating how much harder it was to physically contact someone back then. If you arranged to meet someone and they didn't show, there was no way of knowing if they were just running late or weren't going to put in an appearance at all. And if you went to a festival there'd be huge noticeboards where folk would leave hopeful notes for their friends on the offchance they'd see them: 'Hannah from Basingstoke meet Caroline from Prestwich at the Cider bar at 5pm on Saturday. She will wait for one hour.' This blew my kids' little minds, but the surprising truth is that even though we've never been more connected, with phones and internet and central heating we can switch on while we're out, we are in an epidemic of loneliness.

My job has always given me an insight into the way communities are feeling and changing – when your day job is doing christenings, weddings and funerals, you get a unique picture of what is happening in almost every age group, gender and demographic. One thing I can say with certainty is that over the course of my career I have seen loneliness gradually creeping down through the generations. On the surface you might think it's because we are all so busy – the speed at which we run means it's harder to stop and enjoy the people around us. Or maybe it also has something to do with greater social mobility: whereas generations of the same family used to grow up within a few streets of each other, the younger gener-ation move away from quiet suburbia as soon as they can to live up the high life in London, or as far away as pos-sible on the other side of the world. Of course, this isn't the case for every community, but I think irrespective of where or how we're living, there's something deeper going on and we need to talk about it. If this speaks to you, I hope this chapter helps to make sense of that feel-ing so that you can find your way through it. You are not alone.

A friend to all

It was always expected that part of the job of being a vicar was to comfort people who were lonely because they had lost their partner, or older people who had lost lots of their friends. I've lost count of how many wid-ows I must have visited over the years; there's no escaping the fact that, as a rule, men die younger than women. In their departure, the fellas leave their wives behind them, often women whose lives have been dedicated to looking after their husbands and families. They find themselves alone and without purpose, in the empty family home or else they are moved to somewhere new and unfamiliar. Lots will sign up for clubs and societies like the Women's Institute or the University of the Third Age, and this will help foster friendships, but for many it is like sticking a plaster on a broken leg. Not even the best homemade jam can truly fill the gap left by a loved one. In fact, one widow I met told me that she'd realized that trying to fight her loneliness was futile, she felt it was better to feel it and make friends with it, just like grief. To notice when it's in the room, acknowledge it, audibly if necessary, and sit with it. You can't make it your friend, but you may just be able to get it to sit and be quiet. I thought this was good advice.

I don't say this to put a dampener on things; like everything in this book I think we need to get better at understanding and processing the realities of life. Losing your partner after decades together is unimaginably hard and, like all the challenges we face, deserves to be acknowledged for what it is. But as the years have gone on, the burden of loneliness seems to increasingly affect every generation. It's no longer the sole experience of the elderly, so I've learned to look beyond these external signifiers of loneliness. I've spoken to young people who have hundreds of friends on Instagram but feel utterly isolated. Fathers who feel 'pushed out' when they have children. New mothers who feel cut off and alone at home while it seems like the world carries on without them. People who are part of a minority and feel alone at work because there's no one else like them. It's not necessarily the physical lack of other human beings around that causes it, but a pervading sense of isolation that is often overwhelming. Regardless of your age, class, ethnicity or sexuality, it doesn't matter if you see hundreds of people in a week or you haven't spoken to another human in a month, you can be lonely in a crowded room or perfectly content on your own.

I'm glad when people have the strength to tell me they are feeling lonely, but sometimes they keep it to themselves and I find out the hard way. I knew a woman at one church I worked at, who had nothing to say to me except nasty comments. She sneered while I preached, refused to shake my hand and openly mocked me in front of the congregation. After the service I'd meet her at the door and she'd criticize my hair, or comment on the ridiculousness of my clothes. She once told me I was getting fat. I was already well-versed in turning the other cheek by this point, but one day I got tired of her side-swipes and said: 'Every time you speak to me, Joan, you only have unkind things to say.'

To my surprise she became tearful, immediately apologized and explained: 'My husband died three years ago and since then all I want to do is be with him. I'm lonely.' Her show of vulnerability took my breath away and made me see her in a new light. She didn't stop being mean to me, if anything she got worse, but at least now I had a hook to hang her hideousness on. I couldn't solve her problem, but it helped me understand why she was so furious with the world.

I've learned to spot that some people display their loneliness physically – they seem wilted. I know that's how I seem when I feel lonely, too. But typically people are more private about this pain than any other, even to themselves, and people struggle to sit with that feeling. They will try to fill the void by 'getting out there' and seeking out as much company as possible, forcing themselves to engage in the hope that the noise will drown out their loneliness. Many families tell me their recently bereaved parent has a new lease of life after the death of their partner. I remember one parishioner who signed up for everything the parish hall had to offer after her husband's death. I'd see her charging through the village, yoga mat under one arm and an easel under the other; she even had a go at burlesque dancing – I mean, good for her, but I couldn't help wonder what happened when she got home, took the nipple tassels and the fishnets off and shut the curtains. The 'keeping busy' solves the problem for a while, but it's also bloody exhausting and often a sign of what is going on underneath the surface.

I'm not sure why we've become so afraid of talking about it. Even now, I bet this chapter is making you more uncomfortable than the rest (yep, I saved the best two till last). Somehow loneliness is stealthy and insidious, it feeds on secrecy and relies on the inertia of others. It's gut-wrenching when someone tells us they are feeling lonely – we feel instantly guilty, like we've let them down, and suddenly there is a burden placed on us to make them feel less alone. And I think herein lies the problem: we are afraid of passing on this baton, of making each other miserable. This is why loneliness lurks in the shadows. We might think of it as grief's bed-friend, but it's just as often found lurking in university halls, busy classrooms and teenagers' bedrooms. In the places where no one wants to acknowledge it.

Lonely or just alone?

I think I experienced my greatest period of loneliness as a new mum. It can be so isolating. Sitting breastfeeding in the rocking chair in the wee small hours was where I felt it most. At the time we lived on one of Sheffield's famous seven hills, and the window of the baby's room (not that she ever slept in it, both kids slept in with us) looked out over the city. It was a glorious view, and if I looked carefully I could see the Royal Hallamshire Hospital, the Children's, the University Arts Tower and countless flats, houses and shops. In the darkness I'd count the lights in the windows and imagine who else was up at this time and why. As the little human in my arms sleepily took their fill, I'd pray for each person awake with me and despite distance and anonymity felt strangely connected to others up with me. It was in these moments that I learned the difference between being alone and feeling lonely, and I've been reminded of this many times since.

A few years back I got a phone call from a very concerned local PCSO (Police Community Support Officer). An older lady had been found wandering along the side of the bypass, and when the police had taken her home they found that her house was as dishevelled as she was. She had no family, they couldn't find anyone else to contact, would I visit? Ever needing to be needed, I went round to share some words of wisdom. But when I got there, Vera was as content as they come, sitting in a pile of old newspapers and perfectly lucid in her thoughts and conversation. I asked how she was, offered to make her a cup of tea and asked her if she needed any shopping doing, and when I got on to the idea that she might like to come to the lunch club or perhaps the Mothers' Union she told me to 'piss off and not come back'. Who was I to argue? Lonely hadn't even occurred to Vera, who was entirely content in her own company.

It's all about the context. There are times in all our lives when we would do anything to escape the sound of our own voice, and others where we crave even just an afternoon on our own – usually when small children are involved. Once, when the kids were little, for my birthday present I asked to be left alone and not touched for a morning. I was oversaturated with contact, tired of being the instigator, cheerleader and decision-maker for everyone in the family, even the dog. Responsibility – whether it is parental or professional – can be exhausting and isolating. I didn't even want to be responsible for myself that day, let alone anyone else. And I felt lonelier being mauled by small children than I did enjoying the peace of my own bed, alone.

In the Bible there are plenty of examples of the holy finding themselves alone that demonstrate the import-ance of solitude, but the obvious one is when Jesus spends forty days and forty nights in the wilderness at the very start of his mission, completely alone. It's here, just after his baptism by his cousin in the Jordan river, that his true vocation is realized and he returns a changed man. This story shows how time alone is formative, it helps you reflect on the past and present and prepares you for the job ahead.

We all need time by ourselves to rest and recuperate, so feeling at once surrounded and yet alone when you're a mum can be very disorientating. This period of my life taught me that cultivating time alone to be com-fortable and at ease with ourselves is crucial before we can connect properly with other people. Although social media and its interminable scrolling gets a bad press, sometimes I wonder if the time out from real life and all its pressures that our phone gives us can actually be a respite of sorts, a benign activity that allows us to retreat from others and replenish our reserves. Maybe this explains why I can so happily lose an hour watching carpet-cleaning videos on TikTok.

At this point I also think it's worth noting the famous words of Jean-Paul Sartre: hell is other people. He's not wrong. The quote comes from a play he wrote about three people who find themselves newly committed to hell – just the three of them locked in a room. They wait patiently for 'hell' to arrive, all the fire and torture and darkness they have come to expect. But soon they realize there is no torture or flames. Eternal damnation turns out to be just the three of them locked forever in a room together. They are all each other's hell. Loneliness is not always solved by company, it's more complicated than that. To suggest to a lonely person that they just need to get out more is like asking someone with depression if they've tried mindfulness or suggesting to an anorexic person that they should eat something. Being with others may help, but it won't cure loneliness. Other people treat the symptom, not the cause.

Food for the soul

As the years have gone by and my kids have grown up from full-on toddlers to equally full-on young adults, I've become more able to embrace and accept my 'shadow side', as Carl Jung called it. I've grown to enjoy and even need solitude in a way I never imagined I would. My favourite time all on my own is at the cinema. I love going to the pictures on my own. The staff at my local cinema recognize me now – I usually wear my pyjamas and don't speak to anyone. I know if I haven't been for a while, I feel like I need a reset. And there's snacks.

While loneliness is a blood-sucking jerk of a vampire to the soul, it turns out that being alone can be a rich place of spiritual nourishment even beyond what the latest Richard Curtis film and a bucket of popcorn can give you. If loneliness is feeling disconnected from others, solitude is having the peace of mind to deliberately disconnect for your own wellbeing and growth. For some, it is a spiritual discipline: there are countless medieval saints who bricked themselves up in monastic cells or fled to hillside caves to deepen their spirituality by having no human contact. And while a soul undistracted by another human being's mundane questions might mean a deeper connection to the divine, it does also mean no witnesses to verify your account of the huge angel that handed you a prophecy or a book (just saying).

Personally, the times when I've been compelled to be alone for the sake of my spiritual health, I haven't found it easy. (A bit like being made to eat your vegetables as a kid – no one is holding my mouth open and forcing it down my throat, but I am reluctantly going along with it because I know it'll probably do me good and also once it's done I can get to the good stuff and then go out and play.) Before I was ordained, I was sent off to a silent retreat for a few days. It's pretty standard practice and although it sounds harsh, you don't have to be silent for the entire time: there are pockets of chat, mostly at the end of the day. But during daylight hours there's study sessions, guided meditations, prayers, worship and time alone. I prepared thoroughly. By which I mean I had ordered a whole load of DVDs (it was in the days before online streaming) and bought a bunch of snacks to take with me. While my more diligent friends spent time in chapel or walking in solitude, I was sub-duvet eating crisps. I figured I wasn't talking so I was keeping the rules, right?

As well as individual alone time there were some group alone time activities too, mostly sitting in a circle and sharing the silence. I think this was even harder than being alone and quiet, the temptation to giggle never far away. I found I couldn't stay in that space for long and so I took to exploring the house. There were a few nuns knocking about (yes, we have them in the Anglican church too), and I'm not sure what training course this particular nun had been on but when I walked past her in the corridor her brief glance seemed to see into my soul. She'd clocked me as a spiritual slacker. She didn't say anything, but that look told me I needed to step my soul up. I rushed back to my room, pulled on my shoes and went for a walk. Up a hill. Two things I hate most in the world – walking and hills. But I needed to prove to myself, and to that all-seeing nun, that I had it in me to be a servant of God. I sat with the sheep for a while, closed my eyes and after a while said aloud, to the God I was about to commit my life to, 'OK, you've got ten minutes.' I can't really articulate what happened in those ten minutes, as it is beyond words, but the best way of describing it is that I felt completely and utterly held, known and loved. I was suddenly full of a warmth and depth of contentment, like I was being smiled on by the universe. And it occurred to me that if spiritually being alone is like this, feeling accepted, comfortable and whole, then spiritual loneliness must be the exact opposite. I think those few minutes have underpinned the rest of my vocation – it's a moment I go back to time and again, it felt like a glimpse of heaven – and it made me want it more and to help as many people as possible find their own version of that feeling too.

That was such a formative experience because it came at such a pivotal moment in my spiritual journey. It felt quite surreal that I'd dusted the crumbs off my clothes (albeit Monster Munch, not unleavened bread) and stepped out into the warm glow of God's light, like I had lived my own little Biblical story (there were even sheep present!). Although this story ticks lots of Biblical boxes, there have been plenty more moments when I have felt close to God in less traditionally 'religious' settings, too. I was recently swimming with a friend in an underground waterfall and my breath was taken away by the force of the water, the noise, the smells, the darkness when we turned our head torches off. The cathedral-like cavern and the power of the water stunned me into silence and moved me to tears. I can only describe the feeling as complete contentment and overwhelming gratitude. This for me was a religious experience, of course, but you needn't call it that if that's not the language you speak. Perhaps there's been a moment in your life where you felt completely content with life, where you felt complete peace and none of the usual worries mattered but only that moment, complete contentment and connection; more often than not, those are accidental and surprising but we can make sure the conditions are right to help them occur. I guess this is what we are doing when we surround ourselves with good friends, or plan spa days, or nights out, or visits to mountain tops, we are questing after those perfectly connected moments.

I guess the most relatable version of a spiritual experience I've had was at Glastonbury Festival. Graham and I had taken a break from the crowds of the main arenas and took ourselves off to the bar at the top of the hill. There we met a gorgeous bunch of humans; one of their friends was having a nap on the grass and, it being a blazing hot day, I was really worried he was going to get terribly sunburnt. I couldn't wake him but his friends took me up on my offer of sunblock and covered his face as best they could. We all then held a sort of vigil over him, providing a human umbrella, until he was ready to wake up. We chatted, we laughed and I had the best afternoon I'd had in ages, experiencing real connection and care. We came together in harmony, in support of a fellow human, and shared a special moment that I will remember forever. It reminded me that, for me at least, there is very little difference between the secular and the spiritual, the religious and the non-religious, it's all one and the same for me. It also made me ponder on the correlation between the huge surge in festival-going that's happened in my lifetime in parallel to the decline in church-going, and the way these events bring people together with such heartfelt kindness and love. It struck me that humans seem to need to find a way to gather and connect in peace, to sing and dance together, in the belief that we are stronger as one. There's even a kind of festival attire these days, all those capes and sparkly headpieces, that reminds me of the robes and ornaments of many religious factions. Festivals, it could be argued when you boil them down to their essence, are a manifestation of our faith in each other.

Glastonbury was the site of another formative experience of connectedness for me. Just before the festival started, while the site was being finished, I was filming in the local area for *Songs of Praise*. The festival is of course always on the weekend closest to the Summer Solstice, so when my visit to the town coincided with the date it seemed like too good an opportunity to miss. Despite the fact I needed to be collared up and camera-ready for 8am, I set the alarm for 3.30am to make the walk up the Tor to watch the sun do her thing. Glastonbury Tor is sacred to so many, including to Christians, as it's one of the potential locations for the Holy Grail. Not only that, nearby is the Glastonbury Thorn (or rather the site of it), a hawthorn tree which, according to legend, was planted by Joseph of Arimathea, who brought Christianity to the area and was the custodian of the tomb of Christ. So Glastonbury has a pretty hefty spiritual pedigree and I wanted to experience it at a key moment in the spiritual calendar. I climbed most of the Tor barefoot, a common practice for pilgrims, and the final few steps I did on my hands and knees. I feared I might be the strangest sight there, a middle-aged vicar, collared up and crawling on all fours in the dark. But I needn't have worried, I was by no means the weirdest weirdo there. A sea of tie-dye, drummers, pagans, witches, lots of Christians and a healthy number of bikers. Countless barefoot children and random dogs. I parked myself down on the grass and waited for the sun. It was a friendly, warm place and folk chatted easily. I found myself silently sitting next to a young man in a world of his own, head to toe in leathers, smoking a spliff and with a shaved head, happy to share the silence. I closed my eyes to pray.

'I know you!' he said.

I braced myself for the inevitable *Gogglebox* recognition, but it wasn't from that programme that he knew me. His grandma was in a nursing home with advanced dementia but every Sunday insisted on watching *Songs of Praise*. Her grandson, my new sunrise buddy, loved to watch it with her. The inevitable 'I'm not religious, but . . .' line followed, and he talked about how despite her not recognizing him or being able to speak much any more, she always managed to find the words for the hymns she loved. I was suddenly overwhelmed. We both held the silence and allowed the tears to come. Then the sun peeked over the horizon and my friend began to quietly hum 'Morning has broken'. I joined in. We didn't speak again but didn't need to, though he did offer me his hip flask and the joint, both of which I declined.

Experiences like this have taught me that the antidote to feeling alone and the beauty of real connection can happen in the most unlikely places, at the most unlikely times, with the most unlikely people. Whether it's at a festival, at the top of a hill (they seem to be pretty good places in my experience) or catching up with an old friend, the key is to open yourself up to connecting with something, or someone, and let the warmth in.

We are tribal

We human beings do love a tribe. It was the way we stayed safe – being part of a group was key to our survival. We like to belong to something. John Donne said: 'No man is an island, entire of itself; every man is a piece of the continent, a part of the main.' He was right. I joined every club going when I was at school. Most of them sports clubs. I am not very good at most sports but that didn't stop me. I only liked tennis if it was doubles. I spent the whole of a hockey match lurking on a far wing, more excited about the team bus home. At university I joined the rugby team. They lined us up on the touchline at the first practice in height order, and as the shortest I was asked if I'd play hooker. (I know, I know, 'before I was a vicar I was a hooker' – the jokes write themselves.) I didn't know what that meant but it was nice to have a title, so I said yes. I was chucked – quite literally – into the scrum on my first match, with a herd of magnificent women, all built like trees. It was a people person's dream. Sport isn't ever only about the game, it's another way to be part of something and to belong. It doesn't surprise me when people say they are 'religious' about a sport.

Religion gives lots of people a sense of belonging, it always has. It's a way for people to gather around common values, beliefs and goals. A way to celebrate and commiserate together. Despite what John Lennon sang in 'Imagine' about 'no religion too', the truth is that if religion ceased to exist, human beings would invent it again anyway. It's a big part of why I started going to church in the first place, all those years ago as a disenfranchised teen who wanted to make friends. Church is a great place for the lonely, or for those who want to keep loneliness at bay. Partly, I think, because of the routine and the sense of mucking in. There's a teamwork to church, much like sport. It happens mostly at the same time every week, people will usually be pleased to see you (unless it's Joan giving me the side-eye, of course), and if you want to become more involved there are committees, activities and groups to join. In fact, the church was where many clubs, from youth club and floristry to singing and sports, were first created. Many of our now biggest football clubs, including Everton, Manchester City and Southampton, started out as church teams, organized by enthusiastic curates and youth leaders. Scouts, Brownies, Guides and Beavers are still often rooted in and run by church members. Rural churches in particular are often short of people to do all the jobs that need doing, so you can be on a rota for flowers, cleaning, handing out hymn-books in no time. There's often coffee after the service and you can make friends and new connections.

Right at the start of my vicaring, I met a widower in the parish who told me that since his wife died he'd been very lonely. So I invited him to church.

'But I'm not religious,' he protested.

'What's that got to do with it?' I replied. 'You don't need to sit alone at home. Come and enjoy the gorgeous building, the flowers, have a sing, meet people, join a committee! It'll keep you busy and you'll make friends who will be thrilled to see you. If you enjoy any of the religious bits then that's great, but if you don't, it'll be me that's not done my job properly!'

People seem to be phobic of the word religious. As if being religious is the worst thing you could be. I get messages all the time. 'I'm not religious but I just like lighting candles in church . . .' It's OK if you are, you know? No one stops a builder in the street and says, 'I'm not a plasterer.' Lighting candles, saying prayers, loving churches, finding those with faith interesting to talk to – guess what? It's all OK!

I know this is putting it rather simply, but I do think the idea that you have to be somehow officially religious to go to church is a bizarre notion. You wouldn't go to a French lesson if you already spoke French, or to the supermarket if you had a house full of food. Maybe you'll find faith if you come, maybe you won't, but you'll probably find a support network and not be so lonely any more. Sometimes belonging to something doesn't mean believing every bit of it. Think of someone who goes along to the golf club socials but can't swing a club: maybe one day they'll have a round, maybe they won't, but they'll take what they love about the organization and others will make them feel welcome and included. Of course I'd love it if everyone who came along to the church Christmas fair decided to be baptized and become a 'full believer', but it's really OK with me if they just want to light a candle and buy a raffle ticket too. You don't have to sign up to all of something to get something out of some of it. You don't have to like every song on the album.

Traditional community organizations like the Insurance Institute, the Women's Institute, political parties, the Rotary Club, the Mothers' Union, and all the other clubs your parents or grandparents might once have been part of have all seen their memberships decline over the years, and I can promise you that's not because the quality of the cakes at the WI isn't what it used to be – their scones are as good as ever. Many of the local branches of these societies have had to close. But I don't think this is because people don't want to belong. What I've witnessed from my ringside pew is an increasing reluctance to be organized or to have to give up our free time. Groups, committees, volunteering – they all mean commitment and work, and people don't seem to have the time to spare any more. And yet at the same time, membership of online groups, whether it's Facebook marketplace, online weight-loss communities, knitting forums (even before Tom Daley made it sexy) or sports fans – they have never been more abundant. I've lost track of the number of groups I'm part of on social media. Maybe you have too? While it's not the same as running the jam stall with your pals at the WI market on Saturday, it does seem to suggest to me that we do still want to belong, it's just that the pace of our lives makes it harder to commit to real-life clubs and societies.

I once did a funeral for a biker. The shout went out on social media and on the day of the service countless Harleys, Honda Gold Wings and ancient Triumphs turned up to see the bloke off to the big bike track in the sky. Many of the people there had never met the person who had died, but their shared passion for motorbikes meant they belonged to each other anyway, and I know a great many new friendships and connections were forged that day in real life. I was reminded again of the power for good that social media and our high-speed connected world can offer. We don't always get the balance right, but it can serve us well and bring us closer together when we use it the right way.

We all want to belong, to have our own tribe, it's just that over the centuries we've let go of one big, shared belief and become fragmented as a result. I'm not here to say everyone in every nation or race or culture should believe in the same thing, it would feel ridiculous to suggest that in today's world (unless you're a Trump supporter, or really want to live in a dictatorship, I guess). But there is, I think, a middle ground, where we can be part of a 'church' and have a faith around that, and be proud of it, whatever it is.

I see this 'frayed edge of faith' all the time when people bring their babies to church for christenings. They want the ritual of the church, the sense of belonging, community and values, but often can't articulate what they actually believe. Some clergy get their knickers in a right twist about baptizing babies of families who aren't regular church-goers, but I'm happy to take the desire for the spiritual at face value. These parents on the edge of organized religion will often ask people who also aren't particularly religious to be godparents and that's fine with me. I'm not so naive as to think that everyone who brings their baby for a christening, or every godparent, ticks the box on the census form that says 'Christian'. And yet I often see this in the awkward shuffle from one foot to another as they stand at the font saying their godparental vows. I think my role is to reassure them that it's OK to be unsure, to not have all the answers. I always tell them that one of the best ways to answer a child's questions is to say, 'I don't know, what do you think?' The job of the godparent is to accompany the child on their faith journey, to simply walk with them through life.

My place in it all

When collecting her Outstanding Achievement Award at the Royal Television Society Awards, the fabulous Sarah Lancashire told a story about a lady she had met at the checkout on Christmas Eve who stopped her to say hello. The lady's opening gambit was, 'I bet you think what you do doesn't matter.' She went on to tell Sarah that she would be spending Christmas Day on her own, but she would have the telly on all day and that would keep her company. I found this story so moving because I think it's often forgotten that although TV might seem like frivolous entertainment to some, it is in fact a powerful source of connection for so many. One of the comments that's often thrown at me (sometimes face-to-face and sometimes on social media) is, 'Shouldn't you be doing your proper job rather than being on telly and radio?' I'm accused of neglecting my vocation to serving others because I'm showing off on the telly. Now of course there may be a grain of truth in those unkindnesses, and I may flatter myself to think that hearing my flat vowels over the airwaves combats loneliness (I know it doesn't entirely), but my hope is that it helps. During the pandemic I was very lucky, I got to go to work. Every weekend I would get into my car and drive to Media City in Salford. A deserted motorway meant a smooth journey and when I got to my hotel it was often just me and a few members of staff. On Sundays I'd sit and broadcast three hours of live radio on BBC Radio 2 (my co-host Jason was miles away in Cardiff but you'd never have known we weren't sat side by side). We made a point not to explicitly mention the pandemic (we'd leave that to the newsreaders), but we chatted and cheered and played tunes. And listeners texted in, not just with birthday shout-outs and dedications but overwhelmingly with, 'Thank you for being there.' I felt useful, and those messages lifted me, too. OK, so I wasn't putting people on ventilators or driving ambulances, but I felt like I was doing something to help build a community, to connect people.

Being a vicar working in the media is an unlikely pulpit to an unusual parish, but I see my telly work and the radio presenting as being as much a part of my vocation as taking formal services, and I'm not the only one. I was recently made an Honorary Canon of the cathedral I was ordained at by my bishop. Being made an Honorary Canon is a bit like being made a prefect or given a headteacher's certificate. So I feel like I have full official approval for my showing-off shenanigans on the telly box.

The *Gogglebox* family is still very much part of my story, too. It's a very popular show and it's so lovely to feel even remotely connected to something that brings so much joy to the country, even having only met a couple of the other families. I remember when we first started, I don't think I'd really thought about what it would be like to be on the telly week in, week out, and I was certainly unprepared for how exposing that was. I direct messaged a few of the other cast members and we chatted on social media just to keep checking in on one another, as it was all so surreal. It's interesting how a shared experience like that, especially one that is so far removed from 'normal' life, means we human beings quickly seek out comfort in others going through the same, in solidarity. And that the bonds formed in solidarity, in the face of life's most challenging moments, are the ones that last the longest. So I'm with that lady at the checkout – it doesn't matter how you create connection, it matters. It's what makes us human.

I am so grateful for the connection and belonging that my job has afforded me, but there are strange things that come with being a vicar in the public eye. Namely that people often want to be friends with you or connect with you, and you get the feeling that it's just because you're 'famous' rather than because they actually like you. A champagne problem if ever there was one, but it can get a bit weird. There's a sense you're being collected and seen as someone's personal trophy; the potential friendship feels unbalanced. Often the person doing the collecting doesn't know they are doing it. I get at least one request a week to do a funeral or a

HAVE A LITTLE FAITH

wedding or a christening service for someone who isn't from my patch and whom I've never met. I'm flattered, of course. And I understand why – these are important moments in our lives and the idea that the 'nice vicar off the telly' might come and look after us and be part of the day is comforting. I appear kind and eager to help (in reality I'm probably not as nice as you think – I never empty the dishwasher, that's for sure), and telly creates a false sense of connection. So I understand when people think I will automatically say yes to doing their grandad's funeral on the Isle of Wight because he used to watch *Songs of Praise* every week, even though I've never met them or their grandad and live hundreds of miles away. Or that I will be happy to travel to Inverness to christen their cousin's baby because they have promised me the spare bedroom at their auntie's house and she really does do a lovely breakfast! I get requests like this all the time. Surprisingly often, people who are not yet even dead yet ask me to be the celebrant at their funeral. This is always a no. I can't promise to do a funeral at an unspecified future date, in an unspecified place at an unspecified time. Who knows where I'll be by the time that person dies? I might be living in Outer Mongolia, have lost my faith or even be dead myself (in which case, see you soon!). Again, I am flattered, but also sometimes slightly bemused. I remind myself that it's people seeking con- nection, at a time when they might be disconnected from the established church and not know any vicars nearer to home. When they are experiencing a kind of religious loneliness they reach out to the one they feel they do know. It's lovely, but it's impossible to say yes to, not only because of the practicalities, but also because I technically can't rock up on another cleric's turf like some sort of super-vicar, only to clear off once the service is done, with no pastoral follow-up or aftercare. Vicars have parishes, areas that are in their care, like school catchment areas – where you live means you get the vicar that goes with your patch, you can't rent a vicar from elsewhere, it's not the done thing and I'm not into spiritual one-night stands! When I was first on the telly on *Gogglebox* I felt terribly guilty about not meeting with everyone who got in touch asking for urgent pastoral support, as if being a visible vicar of the nation meant all of a sudden my parish was the entire country. One funeral company even offered me a job when we were on *Gogglebox*, with a company car, a pension and a generous salary so they could offer funerals nationwide taken by the 'Gogglebox vicar!' That was probably the easiest job I've ever turned down.

I also get requests from lonely people who want to connect with me, not to do a service for them but to meet for a pastoral conversation. The request usually comes via a direct message on social media and talks about having seen me on telly or radio and feeling like I'm someone they could talk to. Again, I don't doubt these are genuine and well-intentioned, or that the person isn't in need. It's flattering, of course, and pleases my fragile, attention-seeking ego. Everyone needs to be needed, right? But there are wonderful people in every parish – vicars and pastoral workers who people would be much better placed to connect with. Sometimes I send a card or flowers and offer to match-make them to a clergy colleague geographically closer who will do them a lovely job.

Like I said earlier, my job is more than just turning up and doing 'the God thing', it's about providing moments of connection that come with feeling part of a community. It's about creating a space for people to belong, to feel part of something bigger than themselves. It takes time to build that, and the roots need to be planted deep in order for the connection to thrive.

The way I think about it is that church used to be the club that most people belonged to, and often what you actually believed wasn't really questioned, either by the people around you or by yourself. It provided a place of connection where everyone benefited from coming together under the same roof. Being a member of something helps us, it makes us feel human, and with the church community shrinking, our communities have become more splintered. Of course, I'm not saying that this is the reason for the loneliness epidemic – there are multiple factors in why we're all feeling so lonely these days and I even accept that (although I love it) social media plays a part in that for younger generations – but I think it's hard to deny the effect this has had on our collective sense of community. What I'm saying is, whether it's attending midnight mass, joining a book club, moped ride-outs, having a season ticket to your favourite football club, or doing the weekly Parkrun, there is nothing better than a group of enthusiastic people with a shared passion and belief. Whether it involves the church or not, find the thing that makes you feel connected and put your faith in it. I promise you'll reap the rewards.

Jo Cox, the Labour politician for Batley and Spen who was so brutally murdered in 2016, once said: 'We are far more united and have far more in common than that which divides us.' She was right. The world is tough, but there is no need for anyone to be lonely, we all want to belong, it's in our DNA. And what unites us all is a need to connect and to have faith, however that might look.

THREE GOOD THINGS

While feeling lonely can be physically, spiritually and emotionally destructive, being alone can be fruitful and nourishing for our soul – we just have to know how to do it right. Here's some ways to cultivate happy and healthy alone time while fostering positive connections for good health:

1. **Cultivate some solitude.**
   What's an activity you always do with others, that perhaps you could try on your own? The cinema, the theatre, take yourself out for dinner. This isn't about being grumpy or isolating yourself,

but about developing strength in your solitude and learning to enjoy time alone.

2. **Try a new greeting.**

Practise this: when you meet someone new, don't ask if they are married or have children or what they do for a living: apart from being predictable, it can also be painful and insensitive and puts too much emphasis on people's status – relationship and professional. Try instead to ask what their passions are, which groups they are part of, and what interests them. If we all start asking more of these questions, we might find that people are more willing to share their churches and faiths, whether it's needlepoint, stock-car racing or plain old Christianity.

3. **Seek out a new group to join.**

Even if you don't feel lonely, connection with others is a basic human need and we should always be open to those opportunities. It could be a shift volunteering at a local food bank, or an online group with a shared interest (my friend likes looking at and sharing pictures of doors and gates – apparently there is a big Facebook group for this!) or a face-to-face group. Don't be too hard on yourself if you can't commit every week – even if you only manage a short commitment you might make valuable new connections.

7. Grief

What I want to say first off is: try not to worry about this chapter. I deal in the business of death day in and day out, and it doesn't worry me, but I forget sometimes that death can be a tough subject for many people. I promise I am going to be very gentle with you. I promise this chapter is going to be OK.

Dr Colin Murray Parkes wrote in his book *Bereavement*: 'The pain of grief is just as much a part of life as the joy of love: it is, perhaps, the price we pay for love, the cost of commitment.' When her husband, Prince Philip, died in 2021, Queen Elizabeth II reminded us of this poignant line in her Christmas Day speech later in the same year. It helps us to remember that grief should not be unexpected, but is a kind of settlement for the wonderful life we have had the privilege of leading.

The chances are that you are already experiencing grief in some form or another. As humans we cannot live our lives without experiencing the pain of grief. Grief is normal, healthy and essential, even if it is also painful. Grief needn't exist in uncharted waters, though, because although everyone's grief is so different, there is also much common ground to be shared.

Grief is probably the most common human emotional state that I come across in my job. I meet a lot of people who are grieving the loss of someone they loved. It's also the emotion I feel most comfortable sitting with. Death and funerals and working with the dead and dying is my favourite part of my job. I know, morbid. But I feel useful in these circumstances. I can do it. To hold literal and metaphorical hands with the dead and dying is something I feel strong enough, and privileged, to be able to do. I don't know if that's just a me thing or if other vicars feel the same way. But when I talk here about grief, it's not only the sense of loss and emptiness and frustration and fear that the people I meet are feeling, it's also about all the things that grief arrives with and grows from: death and dying, funerals and the way we say our goodbyes.

No one gets out alive

As you are probably already well aware, death is shit: utterly and completely rubbish. The worst. The thought that someone we have loved is no longer here is the harshest of realities, and for most of us, most of the time, an emotional disaster. One that is made all the worse by the fact that no matter how many green smoothies we drink or prayers we make, it cannot be avoided or outsmarted.

It's not something that scares me, though. I don't like the idea of pain and suffering, of course. But death itself seems to me to be a daft thing to be frightened of, because, by its very nature, we aren't conscious when it happens. And dying is really normal, you know. It is a common thing. The commonest. It happens to everyone without fail, and yet somehow we don't like to talk about it, before, during or after the event.

Of course, what I want for myself and those I love is to die old and grey and quiet in my own bed, in clean sheets that have been dried on the line that morning and still hold the fresh air in their fibres. But I have to tell you that – as someone who probably witnesses more deaths than the average working mum – I don't see that kind of ending happen very often, and I think it's important that we all become more comfortable with that. Most of the funerals I do are for old people, yes, but they haven't just fallen asleep in the night and not woken up. Death is often messy and complicated, and usually a little fuzzy, a slow and sometimes painful fading of the light. I'm talking here about normal dying, from natural causes, not a tragic sudden event like a car crash or a murder. Normal human dying isn't just old age, though. We are taught that it's normal to die when you get old, but what I mean by normal human death could also mean death at a young age, through disease or ill-health. While that might sound brutal, it is not out of the ordinary. It happens.

No matter when someone dies, even if there have been warning signs, it always comes as a shock, and it's my job to help people deal with that shock. This happens a lot in my work: I get a call or an email from a funeral director asking me to go and visit a family whose loved one has died. I give them a ring, arrange a time. I arrive. Usually they are nervous. I know this because when I pull up in my car they are often standing looking out of the window, or the door opens before I've even got out of my car. I go in and am introduced to people gathered around the room. There's handshakes and hellos, some families hug me, and then I ask where they'd like me to sit. Usually a chair in the lounge, but sometimes conservatories or dining rooms. Often the telly is on and I'll ask if they mind turning it off. I once did a visit where I had failed to realize it was the same time as an England World Cup match (I was young and naive, I wouldn't make that mistake now), and the family was too polite to tell me they couldn't do the time I'd suggested I'd visit. It was clear that the telly wasn't going off, so I thought it best to go with: 'Shall we wait for half-time to chat?' I was passed a can of lager and I watched with them and waited. One gentleman I went to visit showed me through to the kitchen where, as well as the two chairs he'd obviously set out for us, there was another chair in the middle of the kitchen floor. It was completely in the way and blocking any easy passage through the room. 'Don't sit on that chair,' he said, 'that's the chair she sat on while we waited for the ambulance and I'm not ready to move it just yet.' Knowing that was the last place she sat, in the home they'd built together, was something he couldn't let go of. Occasionally a family will invite me to sit in 'their' chair, the loved one's, and that always feels very poignant. When I visit a family my first question is always, 'How are you doing?' and more often than not I'm told that ninety-eight-year-old granny dying was 'just such a shock'. I have to fight an urge to smile. She was ninety-eight, I mean, what did you think was going to happen? But it's true. Even though we've known it was coming, we are never prepared for it. I think it says a lot about our collective perception of death that most people I visit whose loved ones have died – despite living a long, long life – have never spoken to them about how they would like their death to be: if they are in hospital would they like to come home at the end? Would they like to know they are dying before the end? It seems that the living think it's their job to protect the dying from knowing, and the dying think it's their job to protect the living from being upset. This results in everyone pretending that the normal death (and remember death is normal) isn't happening because everyone is too scared to say it out loud.

My experience tells me that using the terms 'death' and 'dying' and all the other associated vocabulary isn't anywhere near as scary as we suspect it might be. Some of us might talk about the kind of funeral we want, but we don't talk enough to those we love about the kind of death we want. Believe me, I've tried. In the pandemic I tried to talk to both my parents about what they'd want if either of them found themselves in ICU on ventilation with no promise of a recovery. I don't think my mum understood what I was asking and my dad simply didn't want to talk about it. When my uncle died, who was like another dad to me really, I remember being with him in hospital during our final conversation and I asked him, 'Are you ready?' I was kicked on the shins by my cousin (his daughter) and told to be quiet. This was too painful a question for her to have in the room. Some people don't want to know they are dying. But I've made my family promise to tell me. I suspect most people who are dying know they are, but don't like to say it out loud. Medical professionals don't always help here. They'll often say 'very ill indeed' but never 'dying'. I think it's much more helpful to use the proper words so that people can come to terms with the reality, rather than tip-toeing around it. It's why I never say passed away or passed or lost or say that someone has left us. They died. Try it – it's not that hard to say!

For many of us, the thought of sitting by the bedside of someone we love while they die is a terrifying thought. There might be words being spoken by professionals that we don't understand, unfamiliar noises, smells and sights. No one actually wants to be there. But I have to tell you, some of the most beautiful moments of my life have been in the presence of someone else's death. And being with someone who is dying, while emotionally difficult of course, and heartbreaking, can be completely and utterly glorious. I buried my godmother during Covid. Her daughter, my cousin, Jayne, sat with her for a lot of the time while she died. Jayne confessed to me that those days were golden. Moments of real joy as her mum's life came to its close. The surprising truth is that deathbeds can be beautiful places. Quiet pools of warmth and reconciliation and forgiveness and calm. People often laugh when they're gathered around a deathbed with other family members. They feel strange for laughing and apologize about it, but there's no need. Humour is one of the best coping mechanisms around difficult emotions, and often when the person dying is slipping in and out of consciousness, normal conversation can be a real panacea for them. I hope I can hear people laughing around my deathbed, it would be a wonderful sound to breathe my last to.

I'm not sure why but I think there's been a sanitization of death, particularly in Western culture. Years ago, and indeed in some cultures still, seeing death and dying was a normal part of everyday life. There didn't used to be funeral directors or undertakers, just someone in a community who took care of these things. Often in rural communities it was a farmer or his wife, used to seeing the passage of life and death and less prone to squeamishness. In other communities it was the cabinet or furniture maker. It started out that they would provide a family with a coffin and slowly they started to look after other details of the funeral too. Even now, you don't have to have a funeral director. The body after death legally belongs to the next of kin, and there actually isn't any rule that says you can't look after the whole thing yourself. But you do need to bear in mind the practicalities of that. Not to be too gruesome, but death can be a messy business.

It used to be that you were laid out on your dining-room table by someone from your community and buried within a day or two (probably to avoid said messiness). Neighbours and friends would pass through to say their farewells to the body (this still happens in some communities – the Irish are especially good at this), and the idea that you could reach your adult life without having seen someone who was dead would be a strange idea indeed. Infant mortality and poor health-care all meant death was less distant from our daily lives.

Nowadays, particularly in British culture, death is less public. My friends who are funeral directors tell me fewer and fewer people are asking to view their loved ones after death. There is this notion of 'I prefer to remember them as they were', and of course what-ever feels right for that person is completely up to them. But I've found that seeing the dead person hasn't pushed out the memory of what they were like when they were alive, and that there is no danger of not remembering them as they were just because I have seen them in their death. Sure, it really hurts, but so it should. My worry is that we try to protect ourselves and those we love from the pain and mess of death perhaps a little too much, and I wonder if that isn't doing us any favours in the long run by feeding our fear of death and dying.

Saying goodbye

I also think it's interesting that there has been a shift in the way people approach funerals, away from what they might think of as a religious funeral, but that still has many of the same hallmarks. The National Funeral Exhibition (yes, it's a thing!) happens every two years, and is the trade show for the funeral industry. It is honestly one of the best days out I've ever had. I went along a couple of years ago, with my friend and personal funeral director, John. (I've booked him in for mine already. I always recommend you use a local, family funeral director if you can. Their experience and community knowledge is invaluable.) Like any industry trade show, the National Funeral Exhibition has all the things you'd expect. You can view all the latest limousines and hearses, and countless coffins. I even had a go in one and shut the lid for a second. I'm not going to know what that's like when I'm actually in one, after all. But also at the NFE is a whole load of weird and wonderful things to be used for 'personalization'. Elvis impersonators, birds of prey, dove releases. (I've done a few dove releases now but never an Elvis, or an owl.) You can have coffins in the shape of Red Bull cans and skips (not for me, but to each their own). I think when someone is dying, or even while they are living, they often have lots of thoughts about what they might like their funeral to look like, and sometimes this is because they want to soften the blow for those left behind, and this is a really kind thing. Funerals aren't for the dead, after all, they are for the living.

I once did a funeral for a birdwatcher who, rather than hymns and pieces of classical music, had birdsong and a coffin painted with pictures of his favourite birds. All I'll say is that three minutes is a long time to listen to a mistle thrush. I also once buried an Australian who had the theme song from the TV series *Skippy the Bush Kangaroo* playing as his coffin entered the furnace. Another man had the theme tune from the cricket playing as he bowled out of the crematorium. But my all-time favourite is the gentleman who had a colourful catchphrase and his family wanted that as part of the service, so they spelled it out in flowers. It was quite a sight as the hearse went down the high street with 'SHIT HAPPENS' in a blaze of pink carnations against the coffin.

In case anyone is wondering, I love a horse-drawn hearse. I'd like one for mine. The last horse-drawn funeral I did, the funeral director asked if I'd like to ride up top from the church to the crematorium. I jumped at the chance. But halfway down the road the funeral director whispered under his breath: 'Rein it in, Bottley.'

I thought he was talking about the horses, but turned out I'd got so carried away up there that I was smiling and waving to passers-by.

With the skill of a veteran ventriloquist he added: 'You're not an effing Disney princess.'

Of course all of these novelties are rooted in kind

thoughts, and with the aim of making the event feel more personal to the deceased, but it's an unfortunate truth that they don't eradicate the sadness everyone is feeling. So often people say to me, 'He wouldn't want us to be sad,' and I can't help but think, well, that's tough, because he's dead and it is sad. In fact, it should be sad, because we loved him and now he's gone. I think we've become a bit funeral-phobic in some ways. I see a lot of people not wearing black nowadays, because it's a celebration of life and all that. I totally understand why people want these things, and most funerals do usually have lighter parts and laughter, but the desire to not be sad shouldn't be an attempt to anaesthetize grief. Grief has a way of finding its way out. It's because it is necessary. More on this shortly.

One of the emerging products in the funeral business that is quickly gaining popularity is the 'no frills' cremation. This is where the body of the dead person is cremated without ceremony or service, with no family or friends present, and the ashes are either scattered or returned to the family. This is often done with good intentions; it's cheaper for one thing, but it also does away with the perceived emotional trauma of a funeral. What tends to happen, though, is that there will be a gathering of some sort, with drinks, a buffet, maybe some speeches, a video montage of the person and some music they liked. A funeral by any other name. I've helped friends at these and they will usually say: 'My dad insisted we didn't have a funeral, so we are just getting a few of us together to tell stories, would you compère for us?' Of course I'm happy to, but it sounds awfully like a funeral to me.

Whatever form a funeral takes, it's right and good that we come together and mark the death of someone, create space and time to remember and to hold them in our memory. This opportunity to say goodbye and have the final curtain drawn on someone's life is so important for the grieving process. I also think it's interesting to see from public mourning how the act of coming together in grief is such a crucial part of the process. After the deaths of Princess Diana and Queen Elizabeth II, this sharing of emotion, laying of flowers, or even gathering in a certain place to 'pay our respects' in silence was cathartic. And again I can't help wondering if, with the decline of church funerals, we are missing out on a deeply held human need to grieve, together in a place where that is accepted. I'm also a great believer in letting children come to funerals if they would like to and allowing them to see the adults around them grieve. In my experience it's the grown-ups that don't want them there for fear of upsetting the children, but children are resilient and can learn so much from seeing their family conquer grief – and they also deserve an opportunity to say goodbye. I always recommend that if the idea of children at the funeral is unthinkable, then the children should, probably, be offered some kind of process of their own in which to say goodbye.

I also think an important part of funerals is to have

a moment to remember the person's imperfections – not everything about someone will be missed. I always ask when I visit the family if there was anything about the person that they won't miss. Sometimes there is a great pain and the death of the person can offer release from that. Sometimes it's my job to help people feel no guilt about being a little relieved that person isn't in the world any more. It's why I try to be careful about calling the deceased a 'loved one', because the truth is, not everyone is a 'loved one' – sometimes they were just a 'tolerated one'.

As you may have learned throughout the course of this book, I'm a firm believer in acknowledging what is really happening. This is no truer than in grief. Avoiding the pain of someone's death doesn't usually work, it always finds an outlet, but it's not uncommon for people to use drinking and drugs to cope. One of the first call-outs I ever went to as a priest was to the bedside of a woman dying of cancer. Her daughter was due to be married, but it became clear that her mum wasn't going to live long enough to see the big day. I did a wedding blessing at the bedside and the daughter wore her bridal gown, so her mum could see her. We buried her mum just a few days before the wedding. The father of the bride was so devastated by the death of his wife, and the thought of doing the wedding day without her was so overwhelming for him, that he had a few drinks the morning of the wedding to take the edge off. Trouble was, he didn't stop, not for months. He preferred to try to numb the pain of bereavement rather than face it square on. Many of us will recognize that feeling of wanting to distract ourselves in other less harmful ways, like keeping busy and putting ourselves to good use. And while there are many practical things that will need sorting out, sometimes it's not because they need doing that we do them, but rather because it stops us dwelling too long in a place of sorrow. Many a wardrobe, garage and cupboard under the stairs has had a good fettle, in the hope of avoiding grief. In the early stages of grief, when our emotions are still so acute and abstract, doing things to occupy our hands can allow our brains the space to process what has happened beneath the surface, until we feel more able to sit with those feelings properly.

The outlook for funerals is the same as for most other church services these days. The number of people opting for them is in decline. But that doesn't mean that the services people *are* opting for are without the language and rhythm of faith. For obvious reasons I don't get to go to many funerals that I'm not presiding over, but my family did opt for a humanist celebrant for my nan's funeral. The argument being it would be good for me to just be her granddaughter in this context, and not the priest. And I agreed. It was lovely to have just one job that day, saying goodbye to my nan. It was also fascinating to watch the celebrant work. As a Church of England vicar, I have to use the set words given by the liturgy. You'll almost certainly know some of these words because you've heard them many times in films and dramas: 'earth to earth, ashes to ashes' and so on. We can have other bits too; poetry, readings, reflections and eulogies, but a Church of England funeral has to contain some of the set prayers for the service. But a celebrant is not obliged in the same way, and I presumed therefore that I wouldn't recognize any of the words used. But the celebrant seemed to have lifted most of the words straight from the prayer book I used too. It seems people still want some of the language of faith, but not necessarily some of the religion that comes with it. I suspect the reason they say they don't want a religious funeral is perhaps because they think they will be confronted with piety or a holier-than-thou priest – I think they want faith but not religion. My experience tells me, though, that even if the religiosity is not appealing, the structure, choreography and rhythm of the ancient prayers bring comfort and familiarity, offering a script and stage directions to their grief. Some of the most confirmed agnostics and even some atheists will allow themselves to find a little comfort in the ritual of religion, and perhaps a glimmer of hope that there might be something of comfort to be found in faith when a loved one dies.

What's next?

People tend to search for meaning when they know death is knocking. Someone wise once said: 'There were no atheists on the *Titanic*' – meaning that when death is biting at your heels, even non-believers tend to hedge their bets and go with the afterlife theory. What's to lose, after all? Certainly for many I've met, chucking a few words skywards in the final moments seems to act as a sort of insurance policy. As human beings, it seems to be in our nature to want to think the end isn't really the end. We want to believe that those we love, including ourselves, continue to exist somehow, somewhere after death.

It's no coincidence, then, that most of the major world religions have a belief in the continuation of life, in some form or other, after physical death. Some have a more detailed view of what happens next than others. There's the Islamic Jannah, described as a garden. Hinduism has the concept of Moksha, where the cycle of reincarnation ceases, the ego is released and ultimate connectedness to the self and the divine achieved (sounds good, right?). And of course in Western popular culture we are bombarded by stories of the bright lights, long tunnels and glowing orbs of heaven.

When it comes to the Christian faith, the Bible ironically isn't much of a brochure for heaven or hell; in fact, it fails to go into much detail about what happens next at all. We get a hint of the shape of things to come with the resurrection of Jesus, and it often comes as a surprise, when I've explained it during sermons, that during the statement of faith said by Christians all over the world (the creed), the 'resurrection of the body' doesn't just mean a belief in Jesus's body coming back to life, but also our own. That's why, incidentally, burial over cremation was favoured by Christians for centuries. How could God resurrect a body if there was none?

There are a few clues in the resurrection of Jesus as to what life after death might be like for Christians. He's still recognizable, still scarred and wounded, different but the same. But the image of what we might think of as heaven: fluffy white clouds, big pearly gates, fat cherubs with wings and harps? That is the result of an evolution of ideas and cultural influences. It's part Michelangelo's ceiling, part Victorian sentimentality and part folklore. And just as folk are often surprised when I say I don't believe God is a man with a beard, or that he sits on a cloud in heaven, they are equally surprised when I say I'm not sure what's next after death. And that it probably doesn't look like what any of us might think it does.

What do I believe? Strange as it sounds, I don't always know. Just that there is something, and that it is love. That often seems to be what the dying feel, too. They're not checking in at an all-inclusive holiday destination, where they get an itemized list of what's on offer. It is more nuanced and mysterious than that. When the time is close, the details don't seem to matter so much.

It's the same with hell. Although truthfully, I'm not sure I believe in hell. I certainly don't believe in a place full of bad people being poked with sticks. My faith has never been pinned to a location, underworld or otherwise. Rather it's something that evolves, changes and informs. I'd much rather worry about the here and now, and about living out my faith in the life I'm in, than worrying about what's next and whether I've done enough to win the luxury holiday of eternity in paradise. It might sound controversial, but it also seems to me that the idea of hell if you're bad and heaven if you're good, so you'd better start behaving or else you'll burn, is a kind of Biblical coercive control. Living in fear of what might happen to you after you die seems to me to be totally out of character with the God I choose to believe in, a God who wants life to be lived in its fullness. Fire and brimstone: I'm not into that.

The truth is we can't know for certain about any of the things that any organized faith espouses, and I'd be foolish to talk about certainty. There's a line in the funeral service that says 'a sure and certain hope'. Think about that for a minute. How can hope be sure and certain? The essence of hope is uncertainty, it is unknown. A square circle, a floating lead weight.

But that's what faith is: a sure and certain hope, both immanent and transcendent, here and now, but also distant and never-ending, a patchwork blanket of the unknown and mysterious. If you are looking to the Bible, faith, or anything religious for certainty about what happens after death, evidence of the afterlife or absolute guarantees, then you are barking up the proverbial tree of errors. That's not what faith is for. There is and never can be a battle between the cold, hard facts of science and the ethereal notions of faith, because they are not and never have been trying to do the same thing. Faith can bring comfort at times of death and suffering. But if you come looking for faith to give you certainties and assurances, you're looking in the wrong place. Faith can't do that.

I think the role of faith during these tough times is twofold. First, it can keep you busy and give you something to do when you might be feeling useless (other than tidying under the stairs). There's often a lot of waiting and watching when it comes to normal human death, and there's only so many word searches you can do before you feel you are ignoring the person dying. A trip to the hospital chapel, saying prayers, asking to see the chaplain, even if there's not been a whisper of religion before this, somehow feels proactive and should bring you comfort. And these aren't just open to fully-fledged collar-wearers like me, those words and distractions are there for all and no one should ever feel bad about that. That's what it's for. Faith brings comfort, it is its biggest gift, it does this by fostering connection with a community and giving a sense of shared purpose but also by helping us to focus on the idea of something bigger than just ourselves and our own problems. It helps us to see the miracle of our place in the universe.

It's important to remember that it's OK to want to

believe something when you are going through tough times. When we are grieving or sitting with someone who is dying or facing our own death, the most important thing is to go easy on ourselves. We instinctively know this, right? We take lasagne to people who are grieving to make sure they eat, we encourage them to get some sleep, we might send them gifts to help them feel better, flowers, chocolates, cards. And faith has the same purpose in those moments. It's a tool we should all have in our toolbox to pull out when we need it most. We might not use a screwdriver for five years before pulling it out to help us get through what we are going through. And it's the same for faith. Keep your toolbox in reach for when you need it most.

Somewhere in our cultural understanding we've developed the idea that those in religious positions of power (vicar sorts) keep a register or a loyalty card system and judge those who haven't accumulated many points. We don't. It's totally fine and understandable to call a chaplain to the bedside and say, 'I don't know why I want you here but I do,' or, 'I don't believe in God but I'd like you to pray,' or, as one man said to me at the bedside of his dying wife, 'We've tried everything, this can't hurt.' You aren't daft, it's OK to want the things of faith, even if you don't want all of it or you don't know why, even if you only want them for a very short while. Faith isn't just a possession of the religious, you can have some too and you don't have to have all of it all the time.

A new perspective

Recently I've had a new insight into grieving. My mum, Margaret, died in January 2023. I was in the room when she died. I'd been in those rooms before, of course, and found myself slipping into professional mode with her. Her dying wasn't the hardest bit, nor was the funeral. I spoke at it but didn't do the service. What's hard is the change of context. What I didn't realize when someone very close dies is that it changes your relationship with others closest to you. Not for better or for worse, it's just different. For example, if Mum and Dad were coming to our house for tea, Dad would phone and say, 'I'm bringing your mum to your house on Friday.' Now he isn't bringing her, he's bringing just himself. It changes his purpose. Where there once was a pairing there's now a solo. I'm still working out the change in relationship with my brother and my dad, how we function as a three rather than a four. I know the twenty or so hours we spent watching her slowly slip away were very special indeed, and I wouldn't have wanted to be anywhere else, but of course that doesn't make her death any easier, it will always hurt, I will always be sad.

Something I can recommend: I've had some little business cards printed with Mum's picture on and her name and dates. Every time someone stops me to express their condolences or to ask me how I am, I give them a 'Margaret Card' and ask them to take her somewhere lovely. She's sat on people's fridges, tucked in the back of phone cases, but she's also been on nights out, a gondola in Venice, skiing in the Alps and one lovely friend took her to the Pyramids. I also tuck her into places, behind the wood panelling in a pub, inside the pages of books and maps for sale. It's been a lovely, funny thing to do and it means that the person I give the card to feels like they are doing 'something', more than offering words. I like that she is still out there, sort of. But as my lovely friend John reminded me, of all the gorgeous places she's been to none of them are as lovely as where she actually is. I miss my mum.

I also found this poem from Louise Erdrich incredibly helpful – a friend sent it to me just ahead of her mum's funeral:

> Life will break you.
> Nobody can protect you from that,
> and living alone won't either, for solitude
> will also break you with its yearning.
> You have to love. You have to feel.
> It is the reason you are here on earth.
> You are here to risk your heart.
> You are here to be swallowed up.
> And when it happens that you are broken,
> or betrayed, or left, or hurt, or death brushes near,
> let yourself sit by an apple tree and listen
> to the apples falling around you in heaps,
> wasting their sweetness.
> Tell yourself you tasted as many as you could.

All grief is valid

My dog is also dying. Now I know a dog is not a person. I love my dog, but I am aware that he is a dog and I don't want to upset anyone by conflating this experience with that of losing a loved one (even though I know there are people who would, and that's fine too). My dog is dying though. Buster is thirteen years old and a rescue dog. If you saw me and Graham on *Gogglebox* you'll probably recognize him, possibly by his unmentionables rather than his face. He always lay next to us, legs akimbo, unaware the entire nation could see him in his birthday suit. I know I'm going to have to make a decision about his end of life very soon, something I'm finding harder to process than I anticipated.

I did some work with my spiritual director about it last week. My spiritual director helps me to work out what I'm feeling and thinking, and where my relationship with God is. And we did some poking around about why the thought of my dog dying is hitting me so hard. The conclusion I landed on, with his help, was that with the death of my dog I don't have any job to do except to grieve. Death has become a professional interest for me and so even when I am involved in a death where I am not doing my priestly duties, I am still in professional mode, unable to separate my professional knowledge and experience from the situation. My mum died, and while I didn't take the funeral, I still read at it and took part in it, and as a professional it was impossible not to see it through my vicar's lens, while also being my mum's grieving daughter. But with the dog, because there won't be any of the usual structures and ceremonies around his death that I am used to, no funeral to arrange or wake to organize, it will take me down a different path. I have no other job but to mourn. Like a wheatgrass shot of pure grief. Will it linger or will it disappear quickly, will it come back in waves, as I'm noticing it does with my mum? You can't control who you grieve for. Many people were surprised by how deeply the Queen's death affected them. I heard person after person say, 'I'm not even a royalist,' but of course it wasn't just the Queen they were feeling sad about. Large-scale public grief can resurrect feelings of other bereavements, and reminds us of our own mortality.

When it came to choosing godparents for my son Arthur, one of the people we chose was Mike, an older gentleman in our church. He was a kind, compassionate and godly man and if one of the promises a godparent makes is to pray for their godchildren, we knew he wouldn't shirk from the responsibility, so although we knew that he wouldn't be Arthur's godfather for very long, we were willing to take what involvement in Arthur's life we could get for as long as we could get it. And we were right, Mike was diagnosed with cancer and died when Arthur was only five years old. I remember trying to explain to my little boy that his godfather had died; I sobbed as I told him the news. Arthur looked up at me with his huge blue eyes and said, 'Oh, OK. Can I have a biscuit?' At first I was disappointed by his apparent lack of reaction. A week later our beloved hamster, Mr Jay Tickles, was found dead in his cage. Arthur cried and cried and cried, a full funeral was requested, an inscribed headstone and flowers laid. Arthur was inconsolable for days, crying not just for Mr Tickles but also for Mike. Grief is grief, it doesn't matter in whose name it is held. When we lose someone there's often such a focus on the day and the build-up to it, jobs to be done, phone calls to be made, planning and prep. Once the 'big day' is behind you there's the actual hard work of the business of grieving.

When I was engaged, my focus was my wedding day, and I gave very little thought to what the ins and outs of our marriage would be. When I was pregnant I thought very little about my parenting, I only really thought about the birth. I wasn't reading books on how to look after teenagers or pre-teens when I had a newborn either. It's a bit like that with death.

The build-up to the funeral is intense, with its ceremony and ritual providing a framework in which we know something of what to do; once that passes, we then face the uncharted sea of living without the person. The song on the radio, the visit to the well-loved place, sometimes even a product on a supermarket shelf they used to love. I know people often go out of their way to avoid talking to those who've had someone die, not knowing what to say. This is particularly true if it was an unnatural death, early or tragic. I find avoiding platitudes and asking open questions is helpful, for example, 'I heard your daughter died. I'm so sorry. Tell me about her?'

Grief is the thing with feathers, wrote Max Porter in his book of the same title. It is a living thing, a bird that can come and go as it pleases, a symbol of trauma and darkness but also of freedom and flight. It can disappear from view in a flash, but you know it's still out there somewhere, and you can't know when you'll see it next. Over time, grief doesn't diminish but other things get bigger around it, and what at one time you thought would consume you becomes something you learn to live with, painful though it is.

What I want you to take away from this (slightly more sombre) chapter is that you can have the stuff of faith around your own death and the death of those you love, without signing up for a lifetime of church-going. No one is going to check a membership card or ask when the last time you were in church was. If we only buried the people who believe all of it, all of the time, we probably wouldn't do any funerals – including most of us clergy. The church doesn't have a monopoly on grief, death and dying any more than it does on joy, love and living.

THREE GOOD THINGS

They say there are only two things you can be certain of in life: death and taxes. I know very little about the ins and outs of tax but I do know a fair bit about death and grieving. I've learned so much from the people I've had the privilege of watching die, and from their families and friends who continue to walk on without them. Here's just three, but it could have been the whole book:

1. **Don't be scared of the dying and the dead.**
   There's a great resource called 'Gravetalk', which is a box of cards containing a series of conversation starters asking questions like: 'How would you like to be remembered?' 'Is it OK for kids to come to your funeral?' You can buy it on Amazon and it's really useful to help you have those difficult conversations and find out what someone wants before it's too late.

2. **When it comes to funerals, trust the experts.**
   You might only organize one or two funerals in your lifetime, so you can't be expected to know how it all works. Look to the people who've done this before. Let them help you. Funeral directors are paid well, and while of course most aren't in it for the money, most are worth every penny. Let them do their job so that you can do yours, which is saying goodbye to the person who has died. You don't even have to open your own car door or remember an umbrella. And stop worrying about the buffet.

3. **Never try to draw a line under your grief.**
It may not ever be over, but you will find it easier to deal with. Having a place to sit with and experience your grief can be really helpful. For many this is a grave or a special place where ashes have been scattered. If you don't have easy access to this sort of location, try creating a place in your home where you can remember those who've died. It can be as simple as a candle and a photo in the hall, or as involved as a hand-decorated memory box full of items with special meanings. The point is that it is somewhere for you to reflect and remember in the way that you want to. (And remember that this goes for supporting others too; no one fully gets over grief, so send a card or a text months or even years later. Not just on the obvious days of birthdays and anniversaries, but out of the blue and unexpected, it will never go unappreciated.)

Amen

Writing this book has not been an entirely easy experience. I'm used to seeing the whites of my audience's eyes (less so in radio of course, but you get the idea). When you're broadcasting or holding a service in church, the feedback – and the approval – is usually immediate. I've learned that when writing a book there's no one to applaud you as you deliver your lines. My audience has mostly been the dog. I know the ambition to write a book is something lots of people have. I don't know if it's coming from a working-class background, or plain insecurity, but the more of the book I've written, the more worrisome the idea of having my name on the cover has seemed.

There is something so frighteningly permanent about it. Spouting my opinions on telly or the wireless or from the pulpit feels more temporary (it isn't, of course, not in the era of social media), but writing it down, I've had to repeatedly ask myself: 'Is this what I actually think?' Which of course has been a useful exercise. I realize now why journalling is such an important tool in therapy. I've found that writing, of this kind at least, is an introverted process and one that hasn't come so easily to this extrovert, external processor. I'm not sure every opinion expressed here is what I'll think in five years, or five minutes. Still, I do often suggest that we all challenge ourselves and step outside our comfort zones. Thank you for coming with me while I stepped very far away from mine.

The challenges of the writing process have been amplified by the death of my mother, Margaret. Mum's death has of course impacted almost every aspect of my life. My thoughts and feelings about so many things have changed. The world is not the same place as when I started writing this. I'm not the same person. I've had to think in new ways about my faith, and the concept of faith in general. I'm still thinking.

Mum was in hospital for five weeks and I was there every day. I understood the distress people go through when a loved one is close to death, and it made me think about the ways in which I (and God) can effectively help people, or not. Although she had been there before, this time felt different. I saw close up the pressures the NHS is facing and the burdens NHS workers are carrying for us all. I felt such gratitude, but also great anger and frustration at the way our society treats the people who look after us in this world. I was reminded of the way we all clapped for the NHS during the lockdowns of 2020, and how it always seemed to me like such a superficial gesture. A way of appearing to be thankful without actually doing anything. I questioned the sincerity of the clapping at the time, given that some of the folk banging their saucepans were the same people whose political bents systematically underfund and undermine the

NHS. As I say, power does funny things to people, in politics as in the church.

The Church of England is also experiencing its own crisis, not only in terms of numbers being down, but one of identity. How long can an institution like this maintain its identity as the nation's church? I try to be optimistic, it's my natural default setting. But I'll be honest, it's hard to continue to defend and be part of an institution that still has such an ambivalent attitude to women and gay people, and still fails to properly acknowledge and make amends for its many abuses of the vulnerable and weak. The church no longer gives me a house, or pays me a stipend or a pension; the work I do for it is on the whole voluntary (I am paid for funerals). Why do I basically do free PR for an institution I'm not always convinced is one I wholeheartedly believe is doing the right thing?

I come back to the same answer: because I have faith. Not only faith in God but faith in the belief of how things could be. I believe in resurrection, that out of the tragedy and the emptiness of death something new, beautiful, and full of life will emerge. I choose hope.

If you follow me on social media you'll see I've been making forays into places plenty of old-school vicars don't tend to go. I'm a telly presenter for one thing. I love my work on *Steph's Packed Lunch* and *Songs of Praise*, partly because I'm a desperate show-off but more because I don't think religious spaces are or should be the sole territory of holiness. And because I love people. I've also been exploring other aspects of spirituality: Graham and I have been on a yoga retreat and apparently had our chakras aligned (I'm still not sure what that is but I bloody loved it). I went to a Sacred Circle, where it struck me, not for the first time, that the singing and lighting of candles and what I could only describe as prayer bore an uncanny resemblance to the religious experience of my own church. Increasingly, I'm using a wider range of the tools of spirituality in my own day-to-day life, whether that's mindfulness and meditation (where are your feet?), or journalling, or whatever I need to do. I'm happy with the idea that being religious and having faith in God doesn't need to be an alternative to these other 'spiritual' things. They can all coexist. Belief being more of a bountiful buffet than a set menu. I haven't lost my Christian faith but it's broader than it used to be, and richer for it.

One of the many unusual perks of my job is getting to know more nuns than most ordinary people. I once asked a nun-friend (different slightly to a mum-friend) what she thought about the new trend for mindfulness. She said, with typically light disdain for my frivolousness: 'Kate, we've been doing that stuff for two thousand years.' And it's true, there's nothing new under the sun.

They're all different things to different people, but the element that runs through all of them is an awareness of something other than what physically makes us human: our minds, our thoughts, our feelings. These practices speak to the idea that we are more than simple, sentient meat. Although I'm still not happy about my body and its proportions, I do know that I am more than the flesh and bone I present as. You are too.

There's also a tendency these days to place the spiritual focus all on the individual. To seek the truth inside yourself, to work on your own mental health, and for anything that makes you feel good to be labelled as 'self-care'. That makes me uncomfortable sometimes. I think we have lost sight of the value of community and the spiritual balm that other people can offer us. One of the great joys for me, of being in church and praying with others, is that moment when I can't find the words for my prayers. I know others around me will carry me until I am able to remember and join in again.

I also like the ritual my faith affords me. I like that the words are there for me in services and I don't always have to worry about what to say or do. I love candles and incense and bells and robes and communion. The movements are gently choreographed to be sacred and familiar. But ultimately, when the frills are stripped back, what I'm seeking and what I'm really finding comfort in is connection, just like you, just like everyone else.

However and wherever you choose to focus your spiritual energy, whether it's as part of your local church congregation or saying affirmations to yourself in the mirror, I can't help thinking there's an unconscious spirituality that every one of us will experience at some point in life. Something that we can't put our finger on and that often catches us by surprise. A concert, a

football crowd, a festival: it might not be named and recognized as a 'proper' spiritual experience but there's a
joy that comes with connecting with something collective, bigger than flesh and blood at these things. My
intention is to keep exploring this kind of faith as well.

Ultimately I can't blame anyone who chooses to get
their spirituality from what feels like a less corrupted
source than organized religion. Perhaps organized religion has become so entwined with patriarchy, misogyny,
slavery and corruption that it's irredeemable. Or perhaps it needs to be reclaimed, by those who can help it
find its soul again. I see it as a house, one that has had a
few too many unhelpful modernizations and extensions
and bits of building work done, and somewhere, when
it's stripped back to its bones, the beauty of its original
features is still sitting there, holding everything up.

This doesn't mean I think all religions and belief sys-
tems are the same, nor does it mean I'm about to join a
coven. What it does mean is that I'd gently encourage
those who've perhaps dismissed organized, established
religions to take a moment to look again. The church
hasn't done that great a PR job for belief over the years,
often being dictators of what another's spirituality
should look like, but as a very wise older woman once
said to me: 'Don't let religion put you off God.'

In one of the very first parishes I worked in, my ver-
ger was a woman called Maureen. The church had a
huge Norman doorway, beautiful, regal and majestic,
but there was also a smaller door around the side of the

church. The second door wasn't wide enough to get a pushchair through. On my first day, I naively unlocked and opened the massive door. Maureen shouted from the other end of the church: 'What are you doing? You only come through those doors when you're dead!'

Too often the church has been reluctant to open its biggest, most beautiful doors to the living. It's my intention to keep those big doors wide open, and to keep pushing against the people who try to close them when the 'wrong sort' of person shows up. Faith is not a VIP area, it's an open house, where everyone can come in, help themselves to as much or as little as they need, share a plate with their neighbour or with a stranger, and feel the simple joy in believing that things are going to be OK, in having a little faith.

Thanks

This feels a bit like I imagine an Oscar acceptance speech would, or that bit at the end of *Popmaster* when they say 'everyone who knows me', and I'm panicking that I'm bound to miss someone out, so if you're not thanked but think you should've been, then, thank you.

To all those who recognize themselves in the stories, named and unnamed, I tried my best to discuss with you what I was going to say or disguise you as best I could; forgive me any transgressions.

Graham, Ruby and Arthur, I'm sorry I've been so difficult to get on with while this was all going on and I'm sorry you had to say, 'Just write the bloody thing,' so many times. To my writer friends who bullied me with such love, among them Jason, Cole and Richard, and the friend who let me sit in their house when mine was too distracting, I may have gone through your cupboards when you were out. Tracey, Anna and everyone at KBJ, who know I panic when I'm scared. Amy and the team at Penguin, and lovely Sarah Thompson my book midwife and doula. To everyone who got excited by this when I couldn't, and those who didn't like to ask how it was going. Face snogs and elbow licks to the Rugby girls, our God families, Greenbelters and the Swimmers, Heather, Sarah, Anna, Annabella, Kat and

Katie. And my smashing radio and telly families, especially the teams at BBC *Songs of Praise*, BBC Radio 2 and Channel 4's *Steph's Packed Lunch*.

And Dad, I love you.